THE CRUCIBLE OF
EXPERIENCE

THE
CRUCIBLE
OF
EXPERIENCE

R. D. Laing
and the
Crisis of Psychotherapy

. . .

DANIEL BURSTON

HARVARD UNIVERSITY PRESS
Cambridge, Massachusetts
London, England
2000

Library of Congress Cataloging-in-Publication Data

Burston, Daniel, 1954–
The crucible of experience: R. D. Laing and the crisis of psychotherapy / Daniel Burston.
p. cm.
Includes bibliographical references (p.) and index.
ISBN 0-674-00217-2 (alk. paper)
1. Laing, R. D. (Ronald David), 1927– 2. Psychotherapy—Philosophy.
3. Existential psychotherapy. 4. Antipsychiatry. I. Title.
RC438.6.L34 B86 2000   99-057332
616.89'14'01—dc21

· · · CONTENTS · · ·

ACKNOWLEDGMENTS

· · · A C K N O W L E D G M E N T S · · ·

This book is dedicated to my students, who showed me how to teach Laing's ideas in an engaging and accessible way without sacrificing conceptual rigor or historical perspective.

I wish to thank my colleagues in the Psychology Department at Duquesne University, especially William Fischer, Paul Richer, Constance Fischer, and Russell Walsh, all of whom read and responded to preliminary drafts in a very helpful fashion. Also, a warm word of thanks to Tom Rockmore of the Philosophy Department at Duquesne, whose prompt and careful corrections on several points will save me some embarrassment, though possibly not as much as he would wish. Next, my heartfelt thanks to Kirk Schneider, director of the Existential-Humanistic Institute, Michael Thompson of Free Association, and Tom Greening of the Saybrook Institute in San Francisco. Thanks also to Theodor Itten of St. Gallen, Switzerland, whose copious comments and suggestions proved invaluable, to Leon Redler and Andrew Samuels of London, and to Douglas Kirsner of Deakin University, in Melbourne. In addition to being readers and interlocutors in this project, their publications have been a source of insight and inspiration.

I wish to thank Cyril Greenland of the Archives for the History of Canadian Psychiatry, and John Robert Columbo, both of Toronto, for their kind, thoughtful, and thorough responses to the penultimate draft of this book. And a very special word of thanks to Anthony Storr of Oxford, whose unfailing encouragement and support over the past ten years have been invaluable.

Thanks also to my editor Elizabeth Knoll, whose tact, patience, and professionalism were sorely tested at times, and to manuscript editor Julie Carlson, whose meticulous eye and knack for phrasing often came in handy. And thanks to John Murray, president, Michael Weber, vice president, and all my colleagues at Duquesne

University for their generosity in extending me a Presidential Writing Grant, which enabled me to finish this book.

Thanks to my students Victor Barbetti, Pam Liden and Demmler Schenk for helping to type and proofread the manuscript. And finally, I thank my wife, whose love sustained me throughout.

THE CRUCIBLE OF
EXPERIENCE

AN ENIGMATIC
MAN

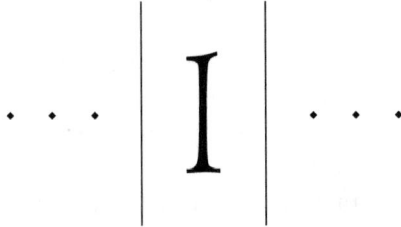

··· I ···

During the last few years, several biographies and books have been published about R. D. Laing, each replete with anecdotes and information that disclose much about this enigmatic man. Laing certainly merits all this attention. More than anyone else in our time, Ronald Laing challenged the mental health professions and society at large to question prevailing models of madness and the nature and limits of psychiatric authority. Despite his outsider status in his own profession, at the height of his career Laing was the most widely read psychiatrist in the world, reaching people across disciplinary boundaries and in all walks of life.

Unfortunately, the controversies that Laing ignited and his own hunger for fame and notoriety focused public attention on his life and personality and away from the actual substance of his ideas. My previous book, *The Wing of Madness: The Life and Work of R. D. Laing,* was an attempt to rectify this unfortunate situation. It traced the origins of Laing's ideas to his personal life experience, and periodized his professional work in terms of dominant themes and issues and contemporaneous ideas and trends. To a lesser extent, it also situated Laing's work in the history of ideas and the mental health professions, with a special emphasis on Laing's relevance to psychiatry and psychoanalysis.

Here I approach Laing differently. For the most part, I scrutinize Laing's work thematically, rather than chronologically, and while I cannot refrain from embellishing on my previous portrait of him, I am sparing with comments about his personality, except where it bears directly on his published work. Furthermore, I dwell much more on Laing's approach to psychotherapy. I am less concerned with his ties to psychiatry and psychoanalysis than with the way his philosophical and religious roots inflect his ideas.

In view of the many books on him of late, I am relieved to say that I still think my previous portrait was on the whole honest, accurate, and sympathetic. Laing was a prodigiously gifted man, but he was certainly no saint. Having noted the contributions of others, however, I do wish to qualify and amend slightly my earlier characterization of Laing.

Ronald David Laing was born on October 7, 1927, in the Govanhill district of Glasgow, a respectable lower-middle-class community. He was the only child of David and Amelia Laing, a quiet Presbyterian couple. Unfortunately, there were deep, divisive tensions between various family members. David's family heartily disapproved of Amelia, whom they felt was an unsuitable companion. Amelia, for her part, felt she had married beneath her station and that David lacked drive and ambition (Laing in Mullan, (1995). In addition, oddly enough, both David and Amelia openly detested their own fathers, rendering their relations with their *own* families problematic. Fistfights between David Laing and his father—Ronald's grandfather—were rare but brutal affairs, and young Ronald witnessed several of them (Laing, 1976).

Another troubling feature of Laing's childhood was the strange relationship between Ronald and his mother. Ronald was born ten years after his parents had married, long after they had ceased having intercourse—or so they insisted. For reasons no one can fathom, Amelia managed to conceal her pregnancy from her entire family until the very day of delivery, suggesting that whatever maternal pride she felt was overshadowed by prudery and shame, and/or a perverse need to keep others in the dark (A. Laing, 1994). And after his birth, Laing reports (1976), Amelia went into a precipitous "decline."

Reading Laing's memoirs, and pondering the impressions of others who knew his family, one gets the distinct impression that Ronald was not a wanted child. Nevertheless, Amelia felt constrained to behave in ways that conformed to prevailing standards of what a mother *should* feel toward her offspring. As a result, while sending Ronald messages that she did not want him or respect his needs and feelings, she also had to disavow the real content of these communications, disguising them as love (Burston, 1996a). So it is no accident that Laing's first book, *The Divided Self*, published in 1960, thematized the problems of *ontological insecurity* experienced by people whose needs, feelings, and experiences are consistently invalidated in early childhood. Nor is it a coincidence that in *The Facts of Life*, sixteen years later, Laing speculated that the majority of people are really unwanted at the moment of their birth, if not, indeed, at the time of conception.

On the whole, Laing's relationship to his father was more supportive and sustaining for Laing than was his relationship to his mother. David Laing was an engineer and ordnance man in the Royal Tank Corps and Royal Air Corps. After coming to loathe his line of work, he gave it up to be a civil engineer for the Corporation of Glasgow. His hero was Mahatma Gandhi, and he was the principal baritone for the Glasgow University Chapel choir. Although he was a devoted family man and a skilled professional, David's passion for music was the emotional center of his life. When Amelia refused to accompany her husband on piano, David started training his son for that purpose, initiating a close musical relationship and an emotional bond between them that would last into Laing's early twenties, and indeed, in some sense, long after David's death. Even in periods of acute distress, Laing was always an intensely musical man (Laing, 1985).

With the help of Julia Ommer, a noted piano teacher, Laing received a licentiate from the Royal Academy of Music at age sixteen—a rare distinction, even today. At school, he excelled in classics and performed splendidly in most subjects. The curriculum did not satisfy his intellectual hunger, however, so at the age of fourteen he resolved to read everything in the local library from A to Z. There he encountered Kierkegaard, Marx, Nietzsche, and Freud for the first time.

At seventeen, Laing enrolled in Glasgow University, and at eighteen, he decided to specialize in medicine. As a university student, Laing was well known for his musical and intellectual gifts, and for introducing his peers to the ideas of Freud. He also helped found the Socratic Club, a debating society that still exists and whose founding patron was Bertrand Russell. Laing's tastes in philosophy were more Continental than Russell's, however, and by age twenty-two, he was working his way diligently through Nietzsche, Husserl, Heidegger,

Sartre, Merleau-Ponty, Jaspers, Wittgenstein, and Camus. The Socratic Club afforded Laing numerous opportunities for discussion and debate, as did his romance with a student from France, Marcelle Vincent, his first love. Indeed, it seems that his romantic and philosophic interludes distracted him from his chosen vocation, because he failed his qualifying exams in medicine the first time around. This elicited so much anguish and embarrassment from Amelia that Laing finally moved out of his parental home at age twenty-three, only to pass his qualifying exams a few months later.

Though military service was mandatory in Scotland, Laing had hoped that his remarkable gifts would help him to circumvent it and study existential psychiatry with Karl Jaspers in Basel. Then he would return to Paris and Marcelle, to hobnob with Sartre and Merleau-Ponty. That was the fantasy, at any rate. Unfortunately for Laing and Marcelle, reality intervened when the military authorities insisted that Laing serve in the medical corps. Laing was crushed. After a brief apprenticeship in neurosurgery at Killearn in 1950, Laing decided to specialize in psychiatry. In view of his earlier interests and activities, this choice was not surprising, but it was vigorously opposed by Joseph Schorstein, a senior surgeon at Killearn who became his mentor in philosophy. Schorstein, like many neurologists even today, held psychiatry in contempt as a barbaric, pseudo-scientific discipline. Next to his ties to Marcelle and his close friend Douglas Hutchison, Laing's relationship with Schorstein was the strongest and most stabilizing factor in his life at that time. From an intellectual point of view, it was absolutely pivotal. With the possible exception of Gregory Bateson, no living person had a comparable influence on his later development.

Laing spent 1951–1953 as an army psychiatrist, differentiating soldiers who were truly disturbed from malingerers. Despite rigid prohibitions on communicating with patients, Laing found ways of developing rapport with genuinely disturbed inmates by sitting quietly with them in their padded cells, often for hours at a time. This move was construed by his superiors as a dedicated research effort—and in a sense, it was. Unlike his peers and superiors, Laing demanded nothing of these lost souls, neither silence nor speech. He allowed them to open up at their own pace, because he wanted to discover how these miserable, frightened, and deeply confused people experienced the world, and how they would respond given the chance to communicate without constraints (Laing, 1985).

In 1952 Laing, age twenty-four and having earned the rank of captain, was placed in charge of the army hospital in Catterick, in Yorkshire. There he met and married a nurse named Anne Hearne. Soon thereafter, he left the army for the Royal Gartnavel Hospital and Southern General Hospital in Glasgow, where he worked under Dr. Angus McNiven, who vigorously opposed electroshock, and his superior, Dr. Ferguson Rodger, who was keen to try innovative approaches. In 1954, Rodger brought Laing to the attention of Dr. J. D. Sutherland, who was then the director of the Tavistock Clinic in London. With the help of Sutherland; his successor, John Bowlby; and Charles Rycroft, Laing, Anne, and their four children came to London in 1956.

During Laing's analytic training, he worked as the registrar of the adult services section at the Tavistock Clinic, and completed *The Divided Self,* a classic in the literature on existential psychotherapy. In 1959, however, as the book went to press, his imminent graduation was obstructed by several members of the training committee, who demanded that he repeat his last year of classes and supervision. The reason, they said, was that Laing had failed to attend the seminars of Herbert Rosenfeld, a powerful Kleinian analyst, and had occasionally skipped others as well. In fact, due to illness, overwork, and a mutual antipathy between Rosenfeld and himself, Laing's attendance had been quite erratic. And though it was not offered as grounds for withholding qualifications, Laing had also cultivated friendly ties with local Jungian groups and made no secret of his leanings toward existential phenomenology—both grounds for suspicion and excommunication among the Freudian faithful. Fortunately, Charles Rycroft, Marion Milner, and Donald Winnicott all leapt to Laing's defense, and he managed to graduate on time (Burston, 1996a).

Meanwhile, one year earlier, in 1958, John Bowlby had introduced Laing to Gregory Bateson's double-bind theory of schizophrenia, which Laing incorporated into his second book, *Self and Others* (Laing, 1961, ch. 7). Laing was intrigued with American research on the families of schizophrenics. With the help of another Glaswegian, Dr. Aaron Esterson, he blended their approach with ideas culled from the work of Edmund Husserl and Jean-Paul Sartre in a study of one hundred such families in the London area. In 1964, Laing and Esterson published some of these cases in a brilliant and deeply disturbing book, *Sanity, Madness and the Family.*

That same year, Laing published *Reason and Violence: A Decade of Sartre's Philosophy* with South African psychiatrist Dr. David Cooper, who later coined the term "anti-psychiatry" (Cooper, 1967a, introduction). Laing always rejected the "anti-psychiatry" label, but regrettably, it stuck. In the ensuing years, friends and detractors alike would think of him as an "anti-psychiatrist."

In 1965, Laing, Esterson, Cooper, and a group of friends and supporters founded the Philadelphia Association, a charitable foundation devoted to the creation of therapeutic communities for people suffering from mental and emotional crises. The Philadelphia Association was committed to the idea that a psychotic breakdown is not a symptom of genetic abnormality or neurological disorder per se, but is an *existential* crisis, and therefore potentially an attempt to reconstitute the self in a more authentic and integrated way. Furthermore, they argued, professional and patient roles, as implemented and understood in mainstream psychiatry, were not conducive to the treatment process. In fact, the roles and procedures commonly used preclude a genuine understanding of the psychotic as a person and tend to confirm the mad in their sense of powerlessness and isolation.

To remedy this situation, Laing and his associates set up therapeutic households to provide genuine asylum from the world outside, a place free from the stigma of diagnosis and the traumas of involuntary treatment. The most famous (and infamous) of these households was Kingsley Hall, in London's East End. As Kingsley Hall took shape, Laing and Anne, who now had five children, became bitterly estranged. Anne attributed their deteriorating relationship to Ronald's intemperate use of LSD, which commenced in 1961 and persisted throughout the sixties. Laing himself blamed the many hundreds of hours he secluded himself from his family to finish his book on families. Either way, to avoid an increasingly explosive domestic situation, Laing moved into Kingsley Hall in 1965, while his wife and children returned to Glasgow. Laing left Kingsley Hall in December 1966 with his new love, Jutta Werner, to launch other projects, but he remained a frequent visitor. Kingsley Hall soon acquired a life of its own and became an integral part of the whole London scene until it closed, finally, in May 1970 (Burston, 1996a).

In February 1967, Laing published *The Politics of Experience*. Though not his best book, it was the most popular, selling more

than six million copies in the United States alone. Due to its spectacular sales, perhaps, Laing achieved more recognition outside
professional circles than he did inside them. One reason for this is
that, like Erich Fromm, Laing cherished a profound mistrust of
psychiatry and the psychoanalytic mainstream, which were still
deeply intertwined in Britain and the United States. Specifically, he
called into question the concepts of normality and adaptation that
most analysts used as synonyms for mental health. A decade before
Laing, Fromm (1955; 1956) had also expressed grave skepticism
about the use of adaptation to society as a criterion of mental
health. Indeed, Fromm wrote about the widespread atrophy of the
ability to think critically, and to feel deeply and authentically in the
face of pervasive "social filters" acquired in the process of socialization (Fromm, Suzuki, and DeMartino, 1960). Unlike Freudian
censorship, which alienates people from the experience of their
own desires but was construed as a purely intrapsychic "agency"
or process, Fromm's "social filters" were logical and linguistic templates embedded in language and the culture as a whole. These
templates shape and constrain our experience of ourselves, of others, and of the world, filtering out raw, primitive elements and
experiences of transcendence. Fromm wanted to transform psychoanalysis from a technique for eliminating symptoms into a humanistic discipline that would access levels and modes of experience
customarily "filtered out" of normal consciousness (Burston,
1991).

Though he did not refer to Fromm in *The Politics of Experience*,
Laing argued in effect that mad people have lost their conventional
social filters and have regressed to a level of development that precedes the acquisition of rudimentary distinctions between self and
other, inner and outer, past and present, real and imaginary, good
and bad, and so forth—cognitive categories that are learned through
socialization, which prescribes commonsense criteria by which experience can be judged valid (or invalid). In Laing's estimation, the
madman's rupture with the "real" (or consensually validated) world
stands in stark contrast to the statistically normal forms of self-
alienation that are usually deemed sane. Unfortunately, normal experiences (or ways of being) are often symptomatic of an equally
radical estrangement from the "inner" world and the mysterious
ground of being—a kind of *pseudo-sanity* masquerading as the real
thing.

In July 1967, Laing participated in the Dialectics of Liberation Conference at the Roadhouse in Chalk Farm, London. The event included most of the leading left-wing and counterculture thinkers and activists of the day (Cooper, 1967b). Laing was extremely disenchanted by this event, and in 1968 began to distance himself from political events, issues, and alliances. This distancing process registers clearly in *Knots* (1970), which, unlike *The Politics of Experience,* steers clear of social criticism altogether. But like *The Politics of Experience, Knots* was also a runaway best-seller.

Despite the spectacular sales of his books, when he finished *Knots,* Laing was burned out and weary of being in the public eye. In addition to running a busy private practice, writing and traveling, and so on, since 1967 Laing had expended vast amounts of energy shepherding the Philadelphia Association, of which he was now chairman, through numerous crises affecting Kingsley Hall and its affiliated households. Accordingly, in 1971 he took himself, Jutta Werner, and their two children to Ceylon (now Sri Lanka) and India for a year. On the first leg of his journey, Laing studied Buddhist meditation at the Kanduboda Meditation Center, near Delgoda, for almost eight weeks. There he meditated for seventeen hours a day under the guidance of an elderly Sinhalese monk, the Venerable Sumatipalo Thera. His teacher was very pleased with his progress, and claimed that Laing had achieved *sotopanna*—a preliminary stage of Nirvana consciousness. Toward the end of September, Laing and family left Sri Lanka for Madras, and thence to New Delhi, where he stationed his family while visiting the Buddhist monastery at Bodgaya. In November, they journeyed from there to Almora, in Uttar Pradesh, where they stayed for seven months. Jutta and the children were stationed at a place called Crank's Ridge, while Laing studied Sanskrit and Tibetan Buddhism. There he communed with a silent, near naked Sadhu called Gangotri Baba in a wooded crevice one mile from nearby Nanital, studying the mysteries of the Indian goddess Kali (Burston, 1996a).

In late March or early April, Laing and his family journeyed to Banaras, and thence to London in April 1972. By all accounts, Laing returned in splendid shape, physically and mentally, although his long absences had put a serious strain on his relationship with Jutta, who feared he would desert her and the children to become a monk or religious recluse. As Laing later confessed to Bob Mullan, her fears were not groundless. Laing *was* deeply tempted to renounce the world and abandon his second family, and her lingering resentment about this caused serious problems later.

Soon after his return, Laing discovered that despite handsome book royalties, he had overestimated his assets prior to his Asian interlude. To avert potential insolvency and embarrassment, he went on a whirlwind speaking tour of the United States, which left him exhausted and probably reeling from the Dionysian revelries in which he indulged between his numerous public appearances (A. Laing, 1994, ch. 16). On his return to London, he learned that Jutta had had an affair while he was away, possibly in retaliation for his many absences over the past two years. Whatever the cause, this disclosure precipitated a crisis that lasted many months. Nevertheless, they reconciled, got married on February 14, 1974, and even had a third child together later that decade (ch. 17).

Having narrowly averted a financial crisis in 1972, and then a marital crisis in 1974, Laing found himself confronted with a new and unprecedented problem—writer's block. Had he relied exclusively on income from patients, this would not have posed a problem. But now he was accustomed to living lavishly off of book sales and reluctant to resume an intensive practice (Laing, A., 1994; Clay, 1996, ch. 15). Unfortunately, Laing's faltering creativity came at a time when sales were dropping steadily and his public reputation was beginning to wane.

To rectify these problems, Laing started developing a new angle on the theory and practice of psychotherapy. But Laing's new angle, to be blunt, was not new at all. As Laing himself confessed, he derived inspiration for this phase of his work from Otto Rank, Francis Mott, E. G. Howe, Arthur Janov, and last but not least, American midwife Elizabeth Fehr, who introduced him to the practice of rebirthing. Perhaps Laing hoped that by putting an original spin on their work, he could capitalize on the emerging craze for birth-oriented therapies that followed Arthur Janov's best-seller, *The Primal Scream* (1970). If so, he was sadly mistaken. *The Facts of Life* (Laing, 1976), his first work on the prenatal experience, did poorly, as did the next book, *The Voice of Experience* (1982), which is a much more thoughtful and engrossing effort than its predecessor.

The seventies were a decade of concurrent and mutually intensifying crises for Laing. At the risk of oversimplifying a very complex situation, his financial crises intensified his marital woes, which in turn stymied his confidence and creativity. Meanwhile, Laing had largely withdrawn from the day-to-day management of the Philadelphia Association and the numerous therapeutic communities that it operated. Though he still functioned as chairman of the organization, it was largely a ceremonial post, and divisions within the Philadelphia Association were becoming acute. As if this were not enough, Laing entered a period of protracted spiritual crisis. Despite his conflicting reputations as a militant atheist, Buddhist, and Yogi, and despite his own avowed penchant for negative theology, for most of his adult life Ronald Laing was a very reluctant agnostic who experienced a great deal of spiritual agony. All of these pressures, operating concurrently, contributed to a deterioration of his personal and professional life.

As the eighties commenced, Laing's marriage and his relationship with the Philadelphia Association grew more strained than ever. While a few members supported him enthusiastically, many regarded his rebirthing phase as either an unwelcome departure from his earlier work, a cynical attempt to win converts, or a way to make an easy buck. Undoubtedly, it was all of those things. But it was also a strange dramatization of some deep inner conflicts.

Many features of Laing's enigmatic personality derived from the fact that he was richly endowed with both a skeptical and a visionary sensibility—attitudes or mentalities that are normally antagonistic to one another. In *The Wing of Madness*, I described Laing's rebirthing phase as a triumph of the visionary over the skeptical mode—at least in his psychotherapy practice, which was frankly shamanistic in character by then. I still hold this view, but with important qualifications. Laing *did* possess both a strong skeptical and visionary sensibility, and the tension between them was a source of tremendous creativity—except in periods of emotional and intellectual stasis, such as during the seventies, when the conflicts between them contributed to his creative paralysis. But a careful reading of *The Voice of Experience*, published in 1982, shows that the visionary mode, which was so strikingly manifest in his shamanistic practices, did not triumph completely—that the creative tension between the skeptical and visionary modes eventually resurfaced. Despite (or because of) its oddly compelling cogitations, few books embody more clearly this kind of creative intellectual struggle.

While finishing *The Voice of Experience,* in November 1981, Laing discovered that Jutta had had another affair the previous year. In fairness to Jutta, in the intervening years Laing had been unfaithful too, but there were aspects of her behavior in this case that shocked him deeply. Jutta, for her part, was thoroughly fed up with Laing's increasingly erratic behavior. They separated soon thereafter. Sadly, Laing's behavior now became so provocative that his colleagues in the Philadelphia Association refused to endorse his re-election as chairman. After a bitter, year-long struggle, Laing left the Philadelphia Association in 1983 and began writing *Wisdom, Madness and Folly: The Making of a Psychiatrist* (Laing, 1985), a memoir that covers the first twenty-seven years of his life. Though illuminating in many ways, the book did not sell, and Laing was unable to recoup his fortunes or restore his intellectual stature. In 1985, Laing joined his former secretary, Margarite Romayn-Kendon, who became his companion for the remainder of his life. They moved to Austria—first to Kitzbühel, and then, in the summer of 1987, to Going. In 1988, Laing met American psychologist Robert Firestone, who invited him and Margarite to join him on his yacht in the Mediterranean. In the midst of a heat wave, on August 23, 1989, Laing, always a fierce competitor, died of a heart attack in the middle of a tennis match.

My first attempt to survey Laing's life and work elicited a wide range of responses. A common one was that *The Wing of Madness* neglected the existential-phenomenological background to his thinking, an omission I rectify here.[1] Another common complaint, even among sympathetic reviewers, was that in likening Laing to Freud and Jung, I had overrated his originality and importance. Perhaps I overstated my case. But unlike Freud and Jung, Laing never started a school or movement to promote and perpetuate his ideas. And as recent developments show, however influential they are at present, Freud and Jung were far less original than is commonly supposed, and far more adept than Laing at concealing the skeletons in their respective closets.

Another concern expressed by some critics—off the record, for the most part—was that I had minimized the extent of Laing's indebtedness to an earlier thinker. Jan Reznek, a former student of Laing's, wrote to me from Perth, Australia, emphasizing Laing's indebtedness to Donald Winnicott. Michael Maccoby, a Washington analyst, noted his extensive borrowings from Gregory Bateson.

R. D. LAING AND
EXISTENTIAL
PHENOMENOLOGY

···| 2 |···

Though trained as a psychoanalyst, Laing's deepest debt as a psychotherapist was to existential phenomenology. As Laing observed to Douglas Kirsner, however, definitions of existential phenomenology are elusive because the major thinkers in this tradition tend to emphasize their differences, rather than their similarities. Edmund Husserl, who called his system "transcendental phenomenology," claimed not to understand *Being and Time,* the crowning achievement of his former disciple, Martin Heidegger. Heidegger, in turn, is rumored to have said that Jean-Paul Sartre's *Being and Nothingness* betrayed a basic incomprehension of everything he stood for. And Sartre, as it happens, had scant respect for Karl Jaspers, who, unlike himself, was a trained psychiatrist as well as a philosopher (Kirsner, in Mullan, 1997).

In addition to strong *individual* differences, like those noted by Laing, there are more diffuse tensions in the field that render definitions difficult. To begin with, there is the religious question. Nietzsche and Sartre were militant atheists, while Kierkegaard, Buber, Tillich, Marcel, Ricoeur, and Levinas were all deeply religious. There are also political tensions. Heidegger was an ardent (if unconventional) Nazi, Buber was a committed (if eccentric) Zionist, and Sartre, though never a Communist Party member, was an avowed Marxist with strong Maoist leanings.

In addition to religious and political divisions, there are tensions between Europeans and Americans. Existential approaches to treatment, which Binswanger pioneered in the early 1930s, did not catch on in the United States until 1958, when Rollo May, Ernest Angel, and Henri Ellenberger published *Existence,* and the Duquesne University programs in philosophy and psychology got under way. As a result, one school claims that to understand existential phenomenology deeply you have to be European, or at least deeply versed in Continental philosophy. Laing was decidedly of this ilk. And another (chiefly American) school of thought argues that it ain't necessarily so.

Finally, perhaps, existentialism and phenomenology have the reputation of being "irrationalist." Irrationalists suggest that the abstract or rational/calculating intellect is not the only path to knowledge of reality—that intuition, imagination, will, and faith are also integral to the wholeness of human experience. The problem with this characterization is that it is usually intended pejoratively. Irrationalism, it is argued, leads inexorably to mysticism or fascism, or some combination of the two. This is sometimes but not always the case. Despite the political extremisms of Heidegger and Sartre, and the incipiently pantheistic tone of Martin Buber's Hasidism, most varieties of existentialism and phenomenology are neither mystical nor totalitarian in tone. Without exception, however, they dispute the normative conception of the human being in which reason *dominates* all other spheres of life. They are not inherently anti-scientific, provided that the natural sciences do not encroach on areas beyond their jurisdiction—for example, ethics, art, politics, and law—or attempt to legislate for them. This was certainly Laing's view. But no matter how it is defined, the "irrationalist" label is simply inapplicable to figures like Husserl, Sartre, and Merleau-Ponty. So Laing was indebted to both the rationalist and irrationalist strains of existential phenomenology—sometimes, we gather later, with slightly confusing results.

That being so, it is easy to see why critics and outsiders are skeptical or perplexed, and why Laing was reticent or simply incapable of generating useful generalizations to describe the spectrum of approaches that go by the name of "existential," "phenomenological," and even "existential-humanistic." Nevertheless, Laing situated himself within this tradition, and since he did not provide us with a suitable starting point for discussion, we have to furnish one of our own.

Existentialism is an approach to philosophy that stresses that despite disparate social and historical situations, differences in age, gender, ability, and so on, all people, by virtue of their mortality, partake of the same basic structure of existence—of throwness, contingency, and the need to infuse or confer value and to impart meaning to life through action and decision, and thus to take responsibility for their personal destiny. The way in which existence is structured—that is, into authentic and inauthentic modes of being (Kierkegaard, Heidegger), into being "in itself," "for itself," and "for others" (Hegel, Sartre), or into various modes of relatedness (Buber, Binswanger, Fromm)—varies markedly from one theorist to another, but the underlying premises about the human condition are often strikingly similar.

Phenomenology is an approach to philosophy that emphasizes that there is a world of immediate or "lived" experience preceding the objectified and abstract world of natural-scientific inquiry. Therefore, fidelity to the texture of human experience, through patient and painstaking description, should precede any effort at explaining the phenomenon in abstract or quantitative terms. Unfortunately, however, in our scientistic culture, we tend to view the world through the prism of multiple abstractions divorced from the foundations of human experience. To regain the freshness of primordial experience, we must unlearn old habits of thought through patient and unbiased attention to the nuances of "subjective" experience, while questioning many widespread cultural preconceptions about organism and environment, mind and body, subjectivity and objectivity, facts and values, perception, memory, affect, volition, and so on.

While existentialism has roots in mid- to late-nineteenth-century philosophy, the term "existentialism" was not coined till sometime in the mid-1940s, apparently by a journalist in France. By contrast, phenomenology (as it is generally understood) was invented at the turn of the century by Edmund Husserl (1859–1938). Husserl was a pupil of Franz Brentano (1838–1917), whose book *Psychology from an Empirical Standpoint* appeared in 1874, the same year as Wilhelm Wundt's *Principles of Physiological Psychology*. Wundt thought that psychology is partly a natural (and therefore experimental) science, and partly a social (and therefore historical/cultural) science. Brentano, by contrast, said that experimentalism is completely unsuited to the study of the mind. Experimentalism studies the behavior of *objects* whose intrinsic properties and overt behavior are not intentional or endowed with meaning, but are the result of impersonal natural laws. Psychology, by contrast, is not about objects, but about mental *acts* (like perception, memory, belief, wishing, willing, and so on), which always refer to the existence of an object outside or beyond themselves—a feature of mental activity he called "intentionality" (Stewart and Mickunas, 1974; Hothersall, 1995). Or as Husserl would say, consciousness is always "consciousness of . . ." You cannot perceive, desire, or believe in the abstract. You invariably perceive, remember, desire, or believe *something*; your consciousness must refer to a specific idea or *content* that directs it at some feature of the world.

One difference between Brentano and Husserl was Husserl's refusal of the subject/object dualism. According to Brentano, consciousness often "intends" external objects that exist quite independently of it. But Husserl insisted that we can never know for certain whether or not objects (or other people) really exist independently of our awareness, because we are only aware of them in and through our own immediate conscious experience (Friedman, 1989). Moreover, careful reflection discloses that the alleged bifurcation between consciousness and its objects is purely abstract and hypothetical. There is no such thing as a content-free consciousness. To talk of the two as if they were separate entities, though commonplace in our society, actually does violence to the facts of experience (Stewart and Mickunas, 1974).

That being so, said Husserl, phenomenological method consists essentially in attending to all the inflections of experience, fully and faithfully, while "bracketing" all naturalistic preconceptions about the "external" causes of phenomena. (The term "bracketing" is derived from mathematics, which Husserl studied before turning to philosophy). This process is also called the "epoche," a term used by the ancient Skeptics and Stoics to denote the "suspension of belief and disbelief." This is much easier said than done, said Husserl, because most human beings are profoundly enmeshed in one or two "prephilosophical" attitudes or orientations, namely, the natural and theoretical attitudes (Stewart and Mickunas, 1974).

In the natural attitude, said Husserl, the individual is engaged in multiple social and "subjective" (affect laden) relationships with the world, and judges reality and the merit of ideas on a purely naive and pragmatic basis—that is, according to whether or not they get results, not whether they represent an "objective" or non-relative truth. The theoretical attitude, by contrast, is based on a naturalistic (Galilean) conception of the universe, in which "objective" truth is actively sought but seen as something that is purged of all subjective qualities and experiences. Indeed, the theoretical attitude is quite wary of appearances and makes strong categorical claims about the manifold differences and relations between appearances and reality (Stewart and Mickunas, 1974).

In the dualistic universes envisaged by the theoretical attitude, there are divergent views about the relationship between reality and appearance. The empiricist position, which was dominant in Husserl's day, is that reality is intrinsically knowable once we have reckoned with the illusory nature of the so-called secondary characteristics of objects—such as their color, smell, taste, and any preferences we have in regard to them—and have focused dispassionately on primary qualities like size, shape, mass, velocity, chemical composition, and so forth. In order to penetrate appearances, say the empiricists, we have to suspend the natural attitude, engage in rigorous measurement and experimentation, and in due course derive from our data a *causal* explanation of events in the world. The Kantian view, which was less popular, was that the alleged primary qualities of objects are also, necessarily, appearances, and that the *Ding an sich*—the thing in itself—forever eludes our efforts at complete comprehension. Accordingly, all our concepts of causality and the structure of things are doomed to be provisional and incomplete, simulations and approximations of the real (Stewart and Mickunas, 1974).

According to Husserl, everything is indeed appearance, as Kant claimed. But the alleged division between the real or noumenal and phenomenal world is a chimera, and reality itself is intimately knowable, provided you approach it properly. Unfortunately, few observers are capable of rigorous phenomenological observation and reflection because they oscillate unwittingly between the natural and theoretical attitudes. And living, as we do, in a scientistic culture, we are apt to accord primacy to the theoretical attitude—in other words, to forget that the ideas and activities pursued within the framework of science are ultimately embedded in and subservient to projects and perspectives derived from the natural attitude— that is, from our subjectivity and sociability. Scientific objectivity, real or imagined, is always established consensually and intersubjectively through the use of communally agreed upon methods of inquiry by people engaged in collaborative and competitive relationships with one another (Husserl, 1970). Whether they acknowledge it or not, scientists are always engaged in passionate and inherently social pursuits.

And what of psychology? Like Brentano, Husserl thought the natural science approach to psychology is completely misguided. In particular, the attempt to derive consciousness from and/or reduce it to the cunning orchestration of various neurophysiological processes is philosophically naive. The most that can be achieved along these lines is physiological psychology. A phenomenological psychology, said Husserl, will be possible one day, when the foundations of phenomenology are more fully worked out. In the meantime, Husserl claimed, it is apparent that consciousness is logically and philosophically prior to any and all of its contents, including the body and the brain. Indeed, in later life, he even ventured to say that consciousness can exist independently of the body, as a disembodied or disincarnate spirit, and waxed eloquent on the immortality of the soul (Husserl, 1970).

Husserl made some extremely large claims, and I cannot do justice to his arguments here. Nevertheless, several things are apparent from this brief summary. First, Husserl's "transcendental ego," which can "bracket" the existence of others but cannot bracket itself, is highly analogous to the Cartesian "cogito." Indeed, Husserl's critics, in and out of phenomenology, argued that it was merely a novel restatement of it, rather than something genuinely new. Husserl responded that, unlike Descartes, he did not ontologize the division between *res mens* and *res extensa*. Fair enough. But while he rejected the dualism of mind and matter that bedevils communal discourse in the natural and theoretical attitudes, he did not transcend it in a convincing way. Instead, he effectively collapsed the latter into the former and insisted that consciousness can exist in complete independence of the body. Since he lacked empirical proof for this position, Husserl relied on logical and experiential grounds to justify it. Despite the eloquence and ingenuity he mustered in its defense, Husserl's idealism was actually the inverse of the reductionist strategy he abhorred so much among materialists. Finally, Husserl's search for absolute certainty, in the form of universal (or transhistorical) and nonrelative truths to ground his "first philosophy," also betoken a decidedly Cartesian sensibility, as Husserl himself acknowledged in *Cartesian Meditations*, which was first published in 1931 (Husserl, 1960).

Husserl's "transcendental phenomenology," as he called it, was fleshed out in a formidable series of books and articles, beginning with *Logical Investigations,* published in 1901, and culminating with *The Crisis of the European Sciences,* published posthumously in 1939. This astonishing body of work, remarkable for its depth and breadth, was neither a finished nor a coherent system—though Husserl had evidently hoped it would be. Nevertheless, it provided subsequent phenomenologists with considerable food for thought. Indeed, complained Husserl, most of them cannibalized his work by assimilating elements of it into new frames of reference that were utterly foreign to him. In the late twenties and early thirties, the brunt of his anger was directed at two former pupils, Max Scheler and Martin Heidegger, and at Karl Jaspers, who was the first to apply phenomenology to the study of clinical psychopathology in a rigorous, systematic way.

Regrettably, in the present context, it is not possible to do justice to Scheler, Jaspers, and Heidegger. Suffice it to say that they blended Husserlian ideas with insights derived from the earlier work of Kierkegaard, Nietzsche, and Dilthey. In an age already bedazzled by its growing technological prowess, Kierkegaard and Nietzsche reiterated the old Socratic view that the true goal of philosophy is self-knowledge and attacked Descartes, Hegel, and the whole rationalist tradition for making inflated claims to omniscience and for being grotesquely divorced from the ground of existence. (For Kierkegaard, this ground was God; for Nietzsche, it was nature or Life). They were scathing critics of collectivism, conformity, and indeed, Christianity; they described the malaise of nineteenth-century Europe as a collective attempt to submerge oneself in "the crowd" (Kierkegaard) or "the rabble" (Nietzsche) so as to avoid individual responsibility. The difference between them was that Kierkegaard (1855) opposed the tepid, complacent piety of conventional religion with the solitude and interiority of a "true" Christian, while Nietzsche, a neo-pagan, rejected Christianity completely as a derivative of "the Jewish slave revolt in morals" (1887).

Another important nineteenth-century influence, on Jaspers especially, was German philosopher Wilhelm Dilthey. Like Brentano and Husserl, Dilthey rejected the naturalistic approach to psychology, arguing that it requires an interpretive or hermeneutic approach. This approach is predicated on discerning the experiences and intentions of people and the way they reflect and engage with their social and historical contexts—their "situation," as existentialists would later say.

The existence (or non-existence) of unconscious mental processes, and their bearing on the mind and the fate of the individual, was a thorny problem for Dilthey. Without turning it into a noun— "the unconscious"—Kierkegaard and Nietzsche nevertheless made ample allowance for unconscious mental processes in their reflections on self-deception and the vagaries of "mass psychology." Moreover, many nineteenth-century thinkers, including Herbart, Carus, Schopenhauer, von Hartmann, and Lipps, had made the concept of the unconscious integral to their systems, though Wundt, Brentano, and Husserl all rejected them and their claims.

Dilthey's rejection of unconscious mental processes was not as consistent or categorical as theirs, however. Like them, he often said that the idea of unconscious mental representations—propounded by J. F. Herbart and adapted by Lazarus and Steinthal in their theory of language—is nonsense. But his remarks circa 1880–1890 are remarkably sympathetic and prescient in several ways. In chapter 9 of *Foundations of Knowledge,* entitled "On Modes and Degrees of Awareness," he wrote:

> The concept of the unconscious representation is often rejected at the outset as self-contradictory. However, the objections are not as such irrefutable. The difficulty is not that a psychic fact cannot be thought of as unconscious in virtue of a generally acknowledged concept of the psychic, nor that a representation is a representation only by virtue of our awareness of it. But consciousness is the way in which a psychic content is there for the ego, insofar as it can be represented at all. Accordingly, an unconscious representation would be an act of being-aware of a psychic content that was not there for the ego. One can see that this is not self-contradictory given a stricter concept of awareness, but it has ramifications that are hard to conceive. Certainly an act of representing that did not involve a direct awareness of something is unthinkable. Thus a *representation* that is *unconscious* must nonetheless be *a direct awareness of a content.* By making this fact clear to ourselves, we find ourselves faced with the idea of a direct awareness which is not itself there for consciousness. This leads to a distinction between lower and higher modes of representing, according to which the ego adds a higher, unified mode of representing

that appropriates the lower mode, which is initially not inwardly there for the ego [and] which can have its effect only from without, like an external stimulus. One can see that such an approach is perfectly consistent with Pfluger's theory about the functions of the spinal chord and its relative autonomy. (Dilthey, 1989, pp. 310–311)

Dilthey noted that a cogent theory of unconscious representation must posit a distinction between higher and lower modes of representation, the lower of which is not directly available to consciousness, but impinges on it from without, as it were, in a quasi-autonomous fashion—a pretty fair adumbration of Freud's primary and secondary processes. Dilthey even tried to give this lower mode of representation a neuro-anatomical location, in the spinal chord, while after 1897 Freud abandoned the effort to localize psychic functions in this way (Ricoeur, 1970).

Still, though he met Freud halfway, anticipating ideas that were not yet in print—and perhaps not yet explicitly formulated—in the final analysis, Dilthey opted for a position like Wundt's. In his own words: "All those facts that are supposed to be explained by the hypothesis of unconscious representations or, more generally, unconscious psychic acts can be explained by psychic acts available as facts in experience whose effects can be confirmed by a variety of instances. These psychic acts are conscious, but not attended to, noticed, or possessed in reflexive awareness. Thus the existence of the unconscious representations or psychic acts cannot be proved on the basis of their effects" (Dilthey, 1989, p. 311).

Despite this resounding refutation, Dilthey also claimed: "The final aim of hermeneutic procedure is to understand the author better than he has understood himself; a proposition which is the necessary consequence of the doctrine of *unconscious creation*" (in Connerton, 1978, p. 116, emphasis added). Yet by Dilthey's own reckoning, hermeneutic understanding is always unfinished, always incomplete. It often transcends the author's limited self-understanding, but in accordance with the Latin maxim *individuum est ineffabile*—a maxim Dilthey loved, and repeated often—hermeneutics can never fully fathom the meaning of an individual author's utterances, which remain shrouded in mystery. The abiding mystery that resides within each of us, beyond the reach of language, as Dilthey thought, is consistent with Laing's musings on the nature of individuality.

In any event, Dilthey's "doctrine of unconscious creation" indicates that despite disclaimers to the contrary, he had not abjured the idea of unconscious mental processes. On the contrary, his approach to hermeneutics was predicated on them. In the aftermath of World War I, however, Freud's work eclipsed the ideas of Dilthey and his colleagues and demanded a cogent response. The first phenomenologist to take up the challenge was Max Scheler. Scheler was an erstwhile disciple of Husserl's who, like Heidegger somewhat later, recoiled from the solipsistic implications of Husserlian thought. His work attempted to apply phenomenology in the realms of feelings and values in ways that Husserl did not endorse. Worst of all, perhaps, Scheler's book *Ressentiment* and his essay "The Idols of Self-Knowledge" affirmed the existence of unconscious mental processes and discussed Freud's work sympathetically. To Husserl, this was a cardinal sin. Like Brentano—who by coincidence, also taught philosophy to Freud—Husserl opposed any theory of unconscious mental processes, and deemed them all so much irrationalist nonsense.[1]

Like his friend Max Scheler, Karl Jaspers affirmed the reality of unconscious mental processes and of various forms of self-deception that are abetted by them. But unlike Scheler, Jaspers thought that Freud's emphasis on sexual repression was symptomatic of bourgeois decadence and lacked deeper anthropological significance. In *General Psychopathology* (1913), a classic textbook in psychiatry, Jaspers described psychoanalysis as a mass movement: a lowbrow popularization of insights articulated earlier, and with more depth and sophistication, by Kierkegaard and Nietzsche. This view was occasionally echoed by Laing (for example, in Russell, 1992, p. 189).

Unlike Scheler, Jaspers was not a follower of Husserl. In fact, his formal training in philosophy commenced only in 1915, although he had applied phenomenological and existential perspectives to mental disorder two years previously, in *General Psychopathology* (1913). According to Jaspers, research on the genetics and/or the neurophysiology of mental disorder ought to proceed in conjunction with the *Verstehende* approach advocated by Wilhelm Dilthey, who wrote extensively about hermeneutics, the role of empathy and imagination in historical understanding, and the historicity of individual consciousness. Indeed, in most essentials, Jaspers' two-track program for psychiatry resembled the program that Wundt had outlined for psychology—part natural science and part cultural, historical, and biographical in character.

Like his friend Max Scheler, Martin Heidegger began as a pupil of Husserl, though he maintained a close relationship with Husserl until 1927, a decade after Scheler broke away. Unlike Scheler and Jaspers, who responded promptly to Freud, Heidegger did not actually read anything by Freud until 1950, and then only at the urging of his friend and follower Medard Boss (1977). Even then, he did not regard the concept of the unconscious as being farfetched or dangerous, so much as misguided and somehow superfluous. As Laing remarked to Bob Mullan, Freud's work is almost trivial from a Heideggerian perspective. To understand why requires a lengthy digression.

Husserl's blueprint for the development of phenomenological psychology involved the patient and exhaustive enumeration of all the potential structures (or acts) of consciousness—perceiving, thinking, willing, feeling, remembering, imagining, and so forth— along with their *intentional correlates* (or corresponding mental contents) and accompanied by precise phenomenological descriptions of their various meanings and conceptual interrelations. Once this laborious project was complete many lifetimes hence, thought Husserl, consciousness would be completely transparent to itself, and complete self-knowledge would be attainable.

Heidegger denied that this was so. Transcendental phenomenology was explicitly intended as a philosophy of consciousness, while Heidegger's "ontological" phenomenology, outlined in *Being and Time* (1927), stressed the primacy of being and the rootedness of consciousness in being. The distinctively human way of being-in-the-world, which Heidegger called *Dasein*, is always somewhat opaque to itself. Different regions or aspects of our being surface for our inspection as we engage in practical commerce with others and with things. But complete self-knowledge is impossible because, until the moment of death, our being is always essentially unfinished. We are always in the process of becoming, of unfolding our latent possibilities, unless we opt for a predominantly "inauthentic" existence.

Heidegger's emphasis on our lingering opacity to ourselves and others was indebted to Nietzsche and Dilthey, but his concept of inauthentic existence was indebted to Kierkegaard and predicated on a tragic sense of life. Like Kierkegaard, Heidegger stressed that from the moment of birth we are hurtling toward death, and that the vivid consciousness of that fact, and of all our as yet unrealized potential, elicits *Angst*, usually translated as "anxiety." The awareness of death calls us to make something of our lives, to take responsibility for our own existence. Those who avoid the call, who seek to evade responsibility for themselves and their fate, allow themselves to dawdle inconsequentially in a hedonistic or pleasure-seeking attitude toward life (Kierkegaard), or to become submerged in the ambiguity and anonymity of Kierkegaard's "crowd"—Heidegger's *das Mann*.

An authentic existence, by contrast, is grounded in interiority and inwardness (Kierkegaard) or in the reticent and resolute bearing of the man who heeds "the call" (Heidegger). But Kierkegaard construed authentic existence as a developmental achievement, a product of ethical resolve and a "higher" level of consciousness that, if allowed to mature to fruition, would issue in a personal relationship with the Almighty. Heidegger, by contrast, was keen to dissociate his concept of authenticity from any ethical or religious overtones. Moreover, and more importantly for our present purposes, Kierkegaard conveyed that the choice to lead an authentic life is an irrevocable commitment that places the individual above or beyond the blandishments of the crowd. By contrast, Heidegger emphasized that the authentic individual is repeatedly swept up in the "hubbub" of *das Mann,* and labors diligently to extricate himself again. So in contrast to the finality that Kierkegaard accorded to authenticity, the circularity of this process, in Heidegger's hands, is indefinite and ongoing.

But regardless of where he finds himself at any given moment, said Heidegger, the individual is never completely self-aware and never incapable of self-deception, of concealing something from himself. According to Heidegger's followers, then, invoking repression, diverse "defense mechanisms," or "the unconscious" to explain these acts of self-concealment does not really *explain* anything. It is not really depth psychology, as its practitioners mistakenly believe, but simply a new language for *describing* a ubiquitous phenomenon, one rooted in a dualistic metaphysics that lacks ontological grounding. In short, said Heidegger and his followers, psychoanalysis fails even as mere description, never mind as explanation (Kockelmans, 1988). This complaint echoes repeatedly through Laing's writings, particularly with reference to psychoanalytic writings on psychosis.

Another thinker who took Freud to task in the 1920s (and subsequently) was Martin Buber. Buber was a pupil of Wilhelm Dilthey and the neo-Kantian philosopher Hermann Cohen. To appreciate his objections to Freud, it helps to contrast his outlook with Heidegger's. In *Being and Time,* Heidegger drew attention to two largely antithetical modes of existence—the authentic and inauthentic. The key issue for Heidegger, as for Kierkegaard, was whether an individual faces his or her fate realistically and is able to experience, express, and unfold his or her potential by living *against* the stream, even if immersed in it (unwillingly or unwittingly) from time to time.

In *I and Thou,* published in 1923, Buber, by contrast, drew attention to the two antithethical *modes of relatedness.* According to Buber, there are basically two ways in which one can relate to others. The I-Thou stance is predicated on mutual recognition and the affirmation of the other person in all his or her uniqueness and difference. It results in genuine "meeting." The I-It stance, by contrast, is reifying or depersonalizing. The I-It mentality regards the person as (1) a means (or an obstacle) to the achievement of one's own desire, and/or (2) a complex concatenation of instincts and/or natural processes governed by impersonal natural laws, whose nature is ultimately reducible to a quantifiable formula.

Contrary to expectation, however, Buber did not say that psychoanalysis is invalid, or even trivial, but that it oversteps its limits and overestimates its strengths. In the clinical encounter, argued Buber, it is just not possible for a healer to really *know* a patient deeply and humanly if the healer's experience is filtered through the medium of theories or categories that fragment the person into a plurality of interacting systems—an id, ego, and superego, for example. And if one doesn't genuinely "meet" the other, one cannot change (or be changed) by the encounter. (More on this point in Chapter 3). Finally, to treat a patient's conscious experiences and intentions as being merely residues of repressed infantile experiences or a palimpsest of unconscious conflicts robs them of their personal meanings and trivializes or evades the problems of personal agency and responsibility. ("My instincts, my upbringing, my parents made me do it!")

Like his erstwhile friend Max Scheler, Buber conceded that at the cultural/historical level, Freud's concepts of repression and sublimation are widely applicable. But unlike Scheler, Buber (1947) contended that they are of central or dominating importance in societies where the I-Thou bond is seriously eroded, and thus where people live their lives in an atmosphere of mutual distrust and uncertainty. In short, said Buber, Freud's attempt to make repression and sublimation "culture-constitutive processes" mistakenly universalizes phenomena that only become pervasive and pivotal when the psychology of the average person is distorted due to the preponderance of relationships governed by the I-It, rather than the I-Thou, nexus.

Despite some similarities, Buber's philosophy hinges on a different set of issues than Heidegger's. The key issue here is not whether the individual resists the blandishments of *das Mann*, but whether he or she is capable of punctuating and invigorating the solitude of the interior life with moments of deep and genuine meeting. For Buber, life consists principally in "meeting," but this deep, joyous sociability is less frequent and vigorous in a society where the I-It mentality prevails. In societies where trust is eroded, people are less willing and, as a rule, less able to risk authentic self-expression and self-disclosure. They flee solitude and sociability alike. The natural dialectic between these states of being is deranged and displaced by an indiscriminate and superficial sociability, as well as by ideologies of extreme individualism, both of which are impoverished and artificial (Buber, 1947; Avnon, 1998, ch. 6).

The violence done to the human soul in these circumstances renders us insensible to our loss of both interiority and meaningful connection. In such societies sexuality and spirituality both suffer. Ideally, said Buber, sexuality and spirituality ought to be vehicles for the experience and expression of the sense of wholeness conferred or elicited in the context of an I-Thou relationship. But absent a "consecration" of the instincts mediated by an I-Thou relation, Buber explained, sexual desire either becomes atavistic and insatiable, or withers, as the act of "love making" becomes mechanical and boring. And where trust is minimal or non-existent, self-disclosure and self-expression become attenuated, and our longing for the sacred becomes contaminated with infantilism and the furtive expressions of unfulfilled desires.

Though never stated in so many words, Buber's critique implied that Freud's mechanistic-hydraulic theory of the libido, and of the infantile and/or Oedipal trends underlying religious ideation, do not describe sexuality or spirituality as such, but rather their distorted and derivative expressions in contemporary life. In other words, they reflect what Erich Fromm would later call "socially patterned defects" or the "pathology of normalcy" (Burston, 1991; Burston and Olfman, 1996).

A more exhaustive comparison between Heidegger and Buber is beyond the scope of this chapter. But two points should be borne in mind. Unlike Heidegger, Buber was admirably crisp and clear in his value judgments. Although his contempt for inauthenticity is palpable throughout *Being and Time,* Heidegger perversely insisted that the distinction between authentic and inauthentic existence is purely formal and descriptive. It was not intended to be *prescriptive*—that is, to elevate one category or way of being above another—or so he claimed. This caveat was in keeping with Husserl's conception of phenomenology as a purely descriptive discipline, and was perhaps his own way of keeping faith with Husserl.[2]

Never having studied with Husserl, Buber had no stake in authenticating his fidelity to him; he infused his analysis of modes of relatedness with the ethical earnestness of Hermann Cohen and the messianic zeal of Hasidism. To the extent that one values human presence, or the human image (as Buber might have said), genuine neutrality is impossible in matters like these. Indeed, any attempt to level the distinction between the I-Thou and the I-It modes of relatedness is an expression not of genuine neutrality, but of mere indifference—an expression, in fact, of a reified (I-It) orientation.

Nevertheless, Buber resembled Heidegger in one important respect. Heidegger noted (contra Kierkegaard) that authenticity is not a permanent transformation or state of being—that authentic individuals lapse insensibly into inauthenticity, only to extricate themselves again. The unstated implication of this position is that the nobler life is one in which we strive for authenticity *as much as possible.* Similarly, Buber recognized that the exigencies of life in the real world preclude a completely "pure" existence—that it is impossible to live without to some extent reifying and being reified by others. Nevertheless, said Buber, a decent and dignified human life is animated by the hope and the effort to deepen and enlarge the sphere of I-Thou relations, at both the individual and societal levels.

Scheler, Jaspers, Buber, and Heidegger offered different orientations and emphases. But their conjoint reflections on the problems of suffering and self-deception; the intrinsic and inescapable historicity of consciousness; and the issues of community, collectivism, and the struggle for authenticity and/or relatedness all prepared the ground for what was later termed an "existential" phenomenology—a term that gained currency in the 1950s. Furthermore, their emphasis on the communal and historical dimensions of existence ensured that phenomenological discourse acquired a social and political dimension—a development that Husserl greeted warily. Surveying Scheler, Jaspers, and Heidegger in the early 1930s, Husserl dismissed their work as irrationalist, as symptomatic of the decay of Western civilization, and as morally and politically dangerous. In retrospect, one can see why. With the notable exception of Buber, they all inherited from Kierkegaard and Nietzsche an aristocratic contempt for democratic movements and institutions. In Jaspers's case, this led to an attitude of complacency, resignation, and political disengagement prior to World War II—though after this conflict, Jaspers became very engaged politically. Scheler, by contrast, was rabidly militaristic during most of World War I, and Heidegger, to Jaspers's evident astonishment, became an ardent supporter of Hitler.

Nevertheless, the work of these philosophers, especially Heidegger's, influenced French thinkers like Jean-Paul Sartre and Maurice Merleau-Ponty in the 1930s. After a lull imposed by World War II, it fed a growing movement that gained momentum thanks to Sartre's literary skills and the remarkable success of *Les Temps Modernes*, the left-wing Parisian journal that Sartre co-founded with Maurice Merleau-Ponty and Raymond Aron.

Transcendental phenomenology still has avid adherents around the world. But the vast majority of phenomenologists favor existential (and/or hermeneutic) phenomenology, which emerged in the 1940s and takes a different approach to the problem of consciousness. Despite his strictures against Cartesian thought, Husserl sought absolute certainty in the cogitations of a disembodied consciousness—a very Cartesian project, after all. By contrast, existential phenomenology insists that the individual consciousness or "psyche" is an elusive entity that is neither separable from nor reducible to the body and its functions, and which cannot be studied (or treated) in isolation from the micro- and macro-social networks in which "it" is embedded. Existential phenomenology attempts to avert what Sartre referred to as Husserl's "disastrous solipsism," and to affirm the *embedded* nature of human consciousness—that consciousness always manifests itself as *embodied* subjectivity and is always historically situated. Another way of expressing this idea is that, in the final analysis, transcendental phenomenology embedded society, the body, and sensuous "appearances" in the structures of consciousness itself, as the "intentional correlates" of our own mental activity (Friedman, 1994). Existential phenomenology effectively reverses this procedure by embedding consciousness in the structures of the body and of society (Stewart and Mickunas, 1974).[3]

It was only natural, then, that during the 1950s and 1960s existential phenomenology engaged in a deepening dialogue with psychoanalysis and Marxism—a conversation with mutative effects on *both* sides of this exchange. The dialogue with psychoanalysis, which deepened after World War II, was prefigured by the intriguing friendship between Freud and the Swiss psychiatrist Ludwig Binswanger. Binswanger was a Freudian stalwart from 1907 to 1923, but abandoned psychoanalysis slowly as he came under the influence of Heidegger, Scheler, and Buber. Binswanger was not unique. During the forties, fifties, and sixties, existentialism claimed the allegiance of many notable men—such as Medard Boss, Victor Frankl, Rollo May, and R. D. Laing—who had trained as analysts but had become disenchanted with Freud and his followers.

Though they were not clinicians, Jean-Paul Sartre and Maurice Merleau-Ponty were also engaged in a fruitful dialogue with psychoanalysis during the forties and fifties, as was Paul Ricoeur in the sixties (Ricoeur, 1970). Merleau-Ponty, in particular, did not stop—or for that matter, start—with Freud. He was well versed in neurology and psychology and integrated perspectives and insights from behaviorism, Gestalt psychology, and medicine in his phenomenology of perception and the "lived body" (Merleau-Ponty, 1964).

The dialogue with Marxism was joined somewhat later, in 1933, by a Russian scholar named Alexandre Kojeve (1902–1968). During the twenties, Kojeve studied with Heidegger; he then taught at the Ecoles des Hautes Etudes Practiques in Paris from 1933–1939. According to Borch-Jakobsen (1991), his pupils included Maurice Merleau-Ponty, Jacques Lacan, Raymond Queneau,

George Batailles, Pierre Klossowski, Alexandre Koyre, Eric Weil, Raymond Aron, Gaston Fessard, Aron Gurwitsch, Henry Corbin, Jean Desanti, and André Breton. Rockmore (1993) thinks that Jean Hyppolite attended the early lectures, and Heckman (in Hyppolite, 1946) adds Sartre and Levinas to the list of participants. In any case, from the tremendous impact and dispersion of his ideas, one gathers that Kojeve's circle was not merely a lively graduate seminar, but a vibrant intellectual community that had an intense and colorful life outside the university. As a result, whether they actually attended or not, Kojeve swayed an entire generation of French intellectuals, many of whom influenced Laing in turn.

Though Kojeve's celebrated seminar was on Hegel and Marx, its primary focus was Hegel's first book, *The Phenomenology of Mind* (1807), in particular the passages on "Lordship and Bondage: The Dependent and Independent Consciousness," or what has since been termed "the master/slave dialectic" (O'Neill, 1996). Because of the extraordinary importance that Kojeve accorded them, and their depiction of the struggle for recognition as the fulcrum of human relations, existentialism and phenomenology after World War II were infused with both a deepening concern with the psychological repercussions of relations of domination and servitude and an element of Hegelian or "dialectical" rationalism that influenced Laing mediately through Sartre and Merleau-Ponty. The impact of Sartre's *Critique of Dialectical Reason* (1963) on Laing is vividly apparent in 1964 (for example, Laing and Cooper, 1964; Laing and Esterson, 1964). But his abiding concern with the issue of domination is evident at every point in his career. Above all, it is reflected in his dissection of the micropolitics of the clinical encounter and of the utter lack of reciprocity and mutual recognition that typically occurs when a patient is deemed psychotic. By Laing's reckoning (1960; 1967; 1987), this clinical attribution usually caps a long succession of micro-political struggles *prior* to the clinical consultation—struggles in which the patient's experience has been routinely invalidated, rendering him an "invalid."

This, then, is a brief sketch of the tradition that shaped Laing's work as a clinician, as evidenced in the footnotes and bibliographies of his books, as well as in his personal correspondence. In conversation with Bob Mullan (1995), Laing recalled which of these thinkers he had encountered when, and which of their books he had read, and so forth, so we need not rehearse those details now. But I will refer back often to the themes and thinkers just mentioned to trace their convergent and conflicting influences on Laing's own work. As a result of Laing's allegiance to existential phenomenology, his relationship to psychoanalysis is complex and ambivalent throughout. His relationship to Marxism is even more complex, and ranged from an attitude of tolerant, even charitable skepticism early on to implacable loathing in later life. Even so, he never denied Marx as a formative influence, though his reflections on contemporary alienation are more Heideggerian in tone.

R. D. LAING AND
EXISTENTIAL
PSYCHOTHERAPY

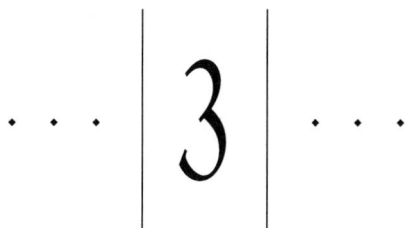

··· | 3 | ···

By virtue of its philosophical underpinnings, which I outlined in Chapter 2, existential psychotherapy is closely connected to Continental philosophy and frames its approach to treatment in light of ideas about the nature of consciousness, community, love, spirituality, and the experience of the sacred. Since 1913, when Jaspers first broached these issues in *General Psychopathology*, it has spawned an extensive and illuminating literature on clinical topics such as anxiety and guilt, depression and suicide, addiction, eating disorders, body image, paraphelias, psychosomatic disorders, and psychosis.

By contrast with existential therapy, "humanistic" psychology is a broad spectrum of approaches native to America that arose in response to Freudian determinism and behaviorism and migrated to Europe in the 1960s and 1970s. Curiously, as Laing's reputation waned during the seventies, many of his staunchest supporters in the mental health field were in the humanistic camp, even though Laing scorned Carl Rogers and Abraham Maslow as derivative and lightweight intellects. So the questions arise: Why were humanistic psychologists so loyal to Laing? And why do they continue to be stimulated and intrigued by his work?

The answer is that despite Laing's scathing remarks, existential and humanistic psychology do have much in common. One conviction that they share, and which influences psychotherapy practice, is the role of self-authorship or self-determination in personality formation. But contrary to popular imagination, this was not a new idea. Aristotle discussed it in the Nichomachean Ethics. And in 1487, in an "Oration on the Dignity of Man," Pico Della Mirandola said that the distinctive attribute of our species—which separates us from animals, on the one hand, and angels, on the other—is the fact that we are free to *choose* whether we are governed by our bestial or angelic propensities. Animals and angels simply are what they are, and lack that choice. Embellishing on the Genesis narrative, Pico has God declare to Adam:

> In conformity with thy free judgement, in whose hands I have placed thee, thou art confined by no bounds; and thou wilt fix the limits of nature for thyself . . . *Thou . . . art the molder and maker of thyself; thou mayest sculpt thyself into whatever shape thouh dost prefer.* (Mirandola, 1494, pp. 4–5, emphasis added)

According to existentialists and humanists then, heredity and environment, instinct and adaptation play important roles in shaping experience and behavior, but they do not necessarily determine what we are or who we become. Our own choices and activities shape our character and condition for good and for ill. But existentialists are also endowed with a tragic sense of life; they qualify their emphasis on self-authorship with both reminders of the inevitability of suffering and tragedy and the element of mystery and paradox that suffuses human life. And like Pico, they note that both "bestial" and "angelic" propensities reside in each of us.

By contrast, noted Laing, humanistic therapists can be quite naive philosophically and may claim, as Carl Rogers does, that human nature is basically good unless or until it is obstructed or tampered with through faulty socialization. Alternatively, they may say that in optimal conditions, human beings strive to realize their full emotional, intellectual, and spiritual potential, and that human happiness is contingent on this process of "self-actualization"—a diluted version of Nietzsche, in Laing's estimation (in Mullan, 1995).

Nevertheless, in addition to their emphasis on self-determination, existentialism and humanism converge considerably in their notions of mental health. In both the existential and humanistic approaches, mental health is emphatically *not* defined by the person's level of cultural congruence or statistical normality ("adaptation" or "adjustment"), but by (1) the quality of relatedness between self and others, (2) the capacity to assume responsibility for one's actions and choices (one's relation to oneself), and by implication, of course (3) the relative preponderance of inner honesty over self-deception.

On first perusal, these criteria of mental health are not particularly striking. But if you reflect long enough, it may dawn on you that one can be completely symptom free, psychiatrically speaking, yet lack the capacity to love deeply, think critically, or choose a position or course of action freely, independently, and responsibly. Conversely, one can be grievously afflicted with psychiatric symptoms and yet be more grounded, authentic, loving, and realistic than someone who is virtually symptom free.

Admittedly, the criteria of mental health that existentialists and humanists share are imponderables—qualities or modes of being that cannot be weighed or measured in a natural-scientific manner. That has led critics to argue that their therapeutic objectives and methods are fuzzy. Up to a point, they are right. But as Laing himself pointed out (1976; 1983), the fact that we cannot explain or measure something yet does not mean that it does not exist, or that it does not have a dramatic impact on our lives. For most of human history, the elemental forces of nature eluded precise measurement. Galileo's break with Aristotelian physics prompted our passion for the mathematization of nature, but it was not until recently that we could measure things like electricity, the weight of atoms, or synaptic activity in the brain.

Are we to suppose, then, that gravity, electricity, atoms, and neurotransmitters did not exist until we could actually measure them and their activity with our instruments? Or that everything real or relevant to human conduct even *can* be measured quantitatively? The answer to the first question is "no." We must suppose that there are entities and processes that exist in nature before we discover how to measure them, otherwise the history of science ceases to make sense. The answer to the second question is moot, however. Can we measure evil, insight, or hope, for example? And can we understand ourselves, or human affairs generally, without them? Existential and humanistic therapists share Laing's conviction that many factors bearing on mental health and disorder probably *cannot* be measured, and that unless or until such measurements are forthcoming, we must reach beyond the more technical job of symptom elimination and ponder the imponderable in the interests of understanding existence.

These facts should be borne in mind as I attempt to distill Laing's answers to the questions "What are the goals of psychotherapy?" and "How are these goals to be achieved?" Two more things should be remembered, however. First, though it is not possible to disentangle them completely, Laing's ideas about individual psychotherapy owe more to the *existential* dimension of this tradition than does his later, phenomenological work with families. And second, while Laing had much to say about the goals of therapy, he scorned the idea of a therapeutic "technique." For Laing, the art of psychotherapy consists in being fully present to the other person without being judgmental, intrusive, or dishonest—a process or a state of mind that he described variously in Buddhist or Heideggerian idioms as, for example, "mindfulness" or "solicitude."

This "one size fits all" approach sounds superficial or even irresponsible to practitioners who advocate a different therapeutic posture for children, adolescents, and adults, for anorexic, borderline, or narcissistic patients, and so on. But rightly or wrongly, that *is* what Laing maintained, though in fact his own clinical conduct varied dramatically according to what the patient needed. The point here is that Laing's therapeutic posture changed according to what he experienced as needed in the moment, during an authentic encounter with another suffering person, and not according to a preconceived theoretical schema (Feldmar in Mullan, 1997).

Finally, remember that while I do my best to formulate Laing's orientation in a coherent fashion, he often questioned whether the critical elements in psychotherapy can be adequately expressed in words. He freely conceded that "there are regularities, even institutional structures, pervading the sequence, rhythm and tempo of the therapeutic situation viewed as process, and these can and should be studied scientifically. But the really decisive moments in psychotherapy, as every patient or therapist who has ever experienced them knows, are unpredictable, unique, unforgettable, always unrepeatable and often indescribable" (Laing, 1967, p. 56).

In short, some experiences elude capture in the net of language, and the effort to do so simply does them violence rather than render them more tangible. In instances like these, no matter how astute or nuanced, verbal formulations may be useless, or worse. At best, they are a tentative approximation, the proverbial finger pointing to the moon.

Laing's first published remarks on psychotherapy appear in *The*

Divided Self, a book devoted to elucidating the dilemmas of the schizoid and schizophrenic patient. Echoing Buber, Laing characterizes psychotherapy as an activity in which the patient's capacity for relatedness "is used for therapeutic ends. The therapist acts on the principle that, since relatedness is potentially present in everyone, then he may not be wasting his time in sitting for hours with a silent catatonic who gives every evidence that he does not recognize his existence" (p. 26).

As *The Divided Self* unfolds, the patient's failure or refusal to communicate is construed as a consequence of "primary ontological insecurity" which renders the patient subject to fears of engulfment and/or petrification by others and a concomitant fear of authentic self-disclosure. Because everyone has a need for authentic self-disclosure, however, the typical schizoid and/or schizophrenic patient is tormented by a constant conflict between the desire to reveal and the desire to conceal (protect) his or her self—a conflict that, as often as not, is *conscious.* To tip the balance in favor of self-disclosure, the therapist must win the patient's trust. To do so, he or she must be nonjudgmental about the patient's idiosyncratic beliefs and behavior. If the patient has a self-schema that precedes physical birth, or even conception, and that survives bodily extinction—for example, if he or she believes in reincarnation—the therapist must not dismiss this idea as delusional, but work empathically *within* that frame of reference to elicit more communicativeness and greater clarity.

Beyond that, echoing Sullivan and Fromm-Reichmann, Laing said that a therapist must draw on his own psychotic potential to understand the patient and insisted that the most important therapeutic agent is the therapist's love—a benignly disinterested love, rather than an erotic *élan* muddied by transference and countertransference. In 1979, in an interview with Andrew Feldmar (Mullan, 1997), he was quite emphatic on this point; he dissociated his concept of love from any theory of libido or desire and likened it to St. Paul's concept of *caritas.* To love someone (or something) "entails letting be, entails seeing and wanting it to be and cherishing it for itself as it is."

Most Americans reading this are immediately reminded of Carl Rogers. The emphases on empathy, being nonjudgmental, working with the client's frame of reference, "cherishing," and so forth all originate with Rogers's "client centered" approach, do they not?

No. As chapter 2 of *The Divided Self* attests, Laing's remarks on empathy, on entering the client's frame of reference, and so on owe more to Wilhelm Dilthey than to Rogers, and his later remarks on love echo those of another Glaswegian psychiatrist, Ian Suttie, whose book *The Origins of Love and Hate* (1935) contained a spirited defense of Sandor Ferenczi's ideas on this same theme. Besides, Rogers's concept of "unconditional positive regard" does not entail a dimension of spirited confrontation and/or a stubborn refusal to gratify a patients' demands for what *they* insist is love.

Take the case of "Mrs. D," whom Laing described toward the end of chapter 3. She had no specific phobias, no vivid panic attacks. But she was perpetually fearful and appeared to be suffering from what is today known as a "generalized anxiety disorder." By Laing's reckoning, Mrs. D suffered from ontological insecurity because since early childhood she had invited or obligated others to confer an identity on her, to define who and what she was and what she could or should do. She made no attempt to define herself autonomously, or in defiance of others' ideas or attributions. In therapy, Mrs. D discovered that despite her extraordinary maleability in this regard, her parents had been deliberately and maliciously inconsistent in their prescriptions and demands—they had been selfish, manipulative, and spiteful toward her. Nevertheless, she identified with her mother, enacting with her children and husband the same sorts of behavior—petty reproaches, constant crying—that she had disliked so intensely in her own mother as a child.

As Laing recalled, Mrs. D was very frustrated by his refusal to treat her maternal identification as genuine and provide her with a new, ready-made identity (or self-schema). Consequently, she developed an intense hatred of him. Rightly or wrongly, analysts would term this a "negative transference," but no matter. Laing felt this development was vastly preferable to colluding with her efforts to perpetuate the past—that is, to avoid taking responsibility for experiencing and expressing herself authentically. As he later remarked in *Self and Others* (1961, p. 123): "It is in terms of basic frustration of the self's search for a collusive complement for false identity that Freud's dictum that analysis should be conducted under conditions of maximum frustration takes on its most cogent meaning."

Many Rogerians take issue here, arguing that the process of engendering lively animosity—whether we call it transference or not—can never be the expression of a loving attitude by the therapist. At various points in *The Divided Self*, however, Laing addressed the necessity of tolerating a patient's hatred as a prelude to evoking a more genuine basis for relatedness (see, esp., ch. 10). And it was in this connection that Laing wrote "the task in psychotherapy is to make, using Jaspers' expression, an appeal to the freedom of the patient. A good deal of the skill in psychotherapy lies in the ability to do this effectively" (p. 61).

While Laing invoked Jaspers here, his position is highly reminiscent of Martin Buber's. In addition to affirmation and respect, said Buber, a genuine I-Thou relation includes an explicit *challenge* to the other to actualize their unrealized potential for genuine meeting, and to tolerate the experience of isolation, emotional dissonance, or distress this might evoke in the other. In other words, a genuine affirmation of the other requires that the other is actually *being* genuine. Buber's chief criticism of Rogers was that "unconditional positive regard" affirms the other indiscriminately (Buber, 1965, app.).

Another obvious parallel here is to the work of Erich Fromm, who described the torments suffered by patients like Mrs. D as the result of a "symbiotic" mode of relatedness. The need for another person to confer or construct one's own identity and to provide authoritative solutions for life's problems at every juncture, as well as the need to identify with such "magic helpers," are described vividly in books by Fromm like *Escape from Freedom* (1941) and *The Art of Loving* (1956). To the best of my knowledge, Fromm never published anything on the clinical handling of such cases, but by virtue of his close affinities with Buber, and his expressed admiration for Laing (Fromm, 1970; 1992), I suspect that his approach was very similar.

Another therapeutic objective articulated forcefully in *The Divided Self* (chs. 8 and 9) is the reduction or elimination of "false guilt." By false guilt, Laing meant (1) a sense of worthlessness or self-loathing occasioned by a patient's inability or refusal to live up to the expectations of others, to be what others say the patient really is (or ought to be), and (2) a more pervasive and diffuse sense of guilt at merely being in the world, brought on by routine parental inability (or refusal) to affirm the child's authentic sense of self. Conversely, *true* guilt emanates from the patient's inability to actualize his or her innate potential for authentic experience and expression—that is, from the failure to be oneself on one's own terms.

In his discussions of "Peter" and "Rose," Laing observed that false guilt prompts the individual to acts of self-negation or self-annihilation, while true guilt, if keenly experienced and acted on, prompts greater self-expression and self-affirmation. The problem with most patients, Laing suggested, is that their guilt feelings are essentially undifferentiated. They are afflicted with a sense of bad conscience, worthlessness, and so on, but experience their self-reproaches monologically, without being able to "hear" the disparate inner voices that attack or belittle them and to understand why. Laing's discussion suggested that differentiating between these "inner voices" is a vital prerequisite to reviving the person's inner core and casting off the emotional "deadness" and isolation characteristic of so many schizoid patients.

It is interesting to note that Laing's analysis of "true" and "false" guilt stood in striking contrast to Freudian theory. Freudians posit only one source of guilt feeling, the superego, which supposedly originates in (1) a phylogenetic inheritance of predispositions that our ancestors acquired in remote prehistory, and (2) the ideals and prohibitions of others, which are internalized during socialization. Either way, however, the superego is equivalent to what Laing termed "false guilt." To illumine his concept of true guilt, Laing invoked Paul Tillich's "courage to be" (1975), which had a profound impact on him. Without belaboring the point, there is a strong parallel between Tillich's "courage" and Heidegger's concept of conscience, of which Tillich and Laing were both well aware. According to Heidegger, the conscience of *das Mann*, or "the *they*," is a "public" conscience that holds the individual responsible for acts or omissions in the public realm. By Heidegger's reckoning, such a conscience is inherently inauthentic and tends to estrange the individual from him- or herself. Authentic conscience calls the individual back to the self to experience the failure to actualize his or her potentials, which include the potential for being with others.[1]

These then are the leitmotivs, in Laing's first reflections on psychotherapy: (1) to elicit and enhance the capacity for relatedness through empathy (Dilthey) and/or love (Ferenczi), (2) to frustrate the search for a collusive complement to the patient's false selves (Buber), and (3) to discriminate between "true" and "false guilt," and to strengthen the former while weakening the latter (Heidegger, Tillich). Another, subsidiary theme in *The Divided Self* was (4) the issue of self-deception, which was first thematized by Scheler and Sartre. Some of Laing's schizoid patients prided themselves on their ruthless inner honesty—that is, on being utterly clear and undeceived about their *own* experiences and motives—even while engaging quite deliberately in deceptive posturing with others. Laing acknowledged the element of truth in this view, arguing that the hypertrophy of self-consciousness characteristic of schizoid people really does confer a greater degree of "psychological mindedness" in them than in the average, relatively unself-conscious individual.

Nevertheless, Laing insisted, some degree of self-deception is intrinsic to the whole schizoid process. The schizoid tendency to route all commerce with external reality through the "false," embodied self, the concerted flight from the corporeal and communal aspects of existence, and so on all necessitate grandiose illusions of imaginary self-sufficiency. The pride one takes in being implacably honest with oneself can be a cover for an ultimately futile flight from relatedness, which Laing did not hesitate to characterize as mad, or incipiently so.

Another, related issue in Laing's early work (and subsequently) is (5) the issue of pretence, which Sartre in particular had dwelt on at some length (1941). In chapter 7 of *The Divided Self,* Laing described an anonymous patient suffering from depersonalization who, as a young girl, had coped with a fear of walking through a public park at dusk by *pretending to blend into the scenery*. This was not unconscious phantasy, but a willful pretence that gave her temporary relief from fear, with the result that, for a brief interval of time, she did not know who or where she was. These adolescent reveries vividly prefigured her adult feelings of depersonalization, and Laing observed (1960, p. 111) that for some such patients "the pretence has been in the pretending and that, in a more real way than he had bargained for, he has actually lapsed into that very state of non-being he has so much dreaded."

To get this vignette into perspective, remember that for schizoid patients, being and non-being, life and death are both the subject of ambivalent longing and dread, but that the longing for temporary oblivion felt by this patient served a specific (evasive) function that briefly stabilized her in some sort of inner equilibrium. Unfortunately, by Laing's reckoning, what began as a conscious strategy for avoiding certain experiences became, by dint of repetition, an involuntary impulse that engulfed more and more of her mental life. Pretence, then, is not a trivial or inconsequential matter for our mental health.

Another therapeutic objective hinted at in chapter 11 of *The Divided Self* is (6) the undoing or overcoming of internal splits. Laing's remarks here, however, were explicitly directed to schizophrenic patients, and therefore perhaps are not applicable to psychotherapy in general. Even so, it is instructive to note that Laing was not referring to splitting in the Kleinian sense, but to Janet's theory of the "molar" and "molecular" splits observed in hysteria and schizophrenia, respectively. "Julie," diagnosed as hebephrenic, was apparently subject to both. But while the discussion of Julie is riveting as clinical description and historical reconstruction, Laing posed an important task for the psychotherapy of schizophrenia without explaining how a real core could be salvaged from the fractured multiplicity of dissociated subsystems within her personality. Even more curiously, on the second to last page he noted that Julie "always insisted that her mother had never wanted her, and had crushed her out in some monstrous way rather than give birth to her normally" (Laing, 1960, p. 204). Laing did not raise this idea again till *The Facts of Life* (1973), when he was no longer focused on schizoid and schizophrenic experience. There he suggested instead that the sense (or memory) of being unwanted, of complicated and traumatic births, and so on can be generalized in large part for patients of all kinds.

• • •

Self and Others, Laing's next book, appeared in two editions. The first, published in 1961 by Tavistock, was subtitled "Further Studies in Sanity and Madness"; the second, revised edition, published by Penguin in 1969, had no subtitle. The second edition of *Self and Others* was revised in light of more recent publications, especially *Interpersonal Perception* (1966) and *The Politics of Experience* (1967), and in anticipation of *The Politics of the Family* (1972). As a result, it reflects more interest in the schematic and algebraic representation of modes of experience that are suffused by unconscious fantasy—or "phantasy," as Laing insisted on spelling it. Even so, in both editions, the problems of self-deception and pretence, which are subsidiary themes in *The Divided Self,* cease being secondary and occupy center stage. Moreover, Laing is no longer focused on people suffering from primary ontological insecurity. Finally, another shift, noted by Douglas Kirsner (1976), is that while *The Divided Self* emphasizes the "inner" world of patients, *Self and Others* dwells primarily on the *interpersonal*. This shift in emphasis is apparent by the end of chapter 1, when, echoing Buber, Laing declared: "The 'unconscious' is what we do not communicate, to ourselves or to one another. We may convey something to another, without communicating it to ourselves. Something about Peter is evident to Paul that is not evident to Peter. That is *one* sense of the phrase, 'Peter is unconscious of'" (Laing, 1969, p. 32).

In fairness to Freud, he did devote some attention to the processes of unconscious communication (Ricoeur, 1970; Burston, 1986). For the most part, however, Freud construed "the unconscious" as an essentially closed system of reciprocally facilitating or inhibiting energetic impulses regulated by the pleasure and reality principles. Though it was never his stated purpose, evidently one of Laing's goals in *Self and Others* was to come to grips with psychoanalysis more deeply and effectively than he had previously.

On the face of it, this was a strange ambition. After all, *The Divided Self* bristled with references to analytic theories, and the majority of clinicians he thanked in his acknowledgments section were analysts. Even so, chapter 1 of *The Divided Self* characterized Freud's theory of the unconscious as "an instrument of defense" (p. 25)—though a defense against *what* was not at all clear. Judging from context, and from his admiration for Heidegger, Laing was probably implying that Freud's account of "the unconscious" is a defense against experiencing the inherent and perhaps intractable difficulty of even *describing* schizoid or psychotic states of mind faithfully without secretly infusing them with a priori theoretical preconceptions. This impression is buttressed by the fact that in chapter 5 of *Self and Others* (1969, p. 75), Laing underlined "the naked, intricate actuality of the complexity of experiences that those of us who do not deny what we cannot explain or even describe are struggling to understand. Theory can only legitimately be made on behalf of experience, not in order to deny experience which the theory ignores out of embarrassment."

Given Laing's recent graduation as a psychoanalyst, it seems likely that this caveat was rooted in his experience at the London

Institute of Psycho-Analysis, and that for a decade or so afterward, his experiences there colored his attitude toward Freud personally (Burston, 1996, ch. 3). Still, Laing never rejected analytic theory totally but incorporated it selectively, when it proved compatible with an existential point of view. Laing's characteristic ambivalence toward psychoanalysis was already deeply engrained *before* his analytic training, as we glean from an excerpt from an undated letter to Marcelle Vincent (ca. 1950).

> In psychiatry: a young man of 28. Married three years ago. One child. A writer. Made a precarious living writing what he wanted to write: good: talented; no sale for his stuff. Took to writing for women's magazines, etc. Making over 2,000 pounds a year, very successful. Recently, can't concentrate on his work: can't get started: irritable: angry and abusive to his wife: remorseful afterwards: losing commissions—comes for treatment.
>
> Now, imaging myself to be his psychiatrist, I could take this view. The fundamental problem is his inability to adapt to his environmental circumstances. He is successful for the first time in his life, comfortable, wife, whom he loves, and a child. He is not sufficiently talented apparently to make a living by genuine literature. He is both unable to accept and assimilate this fact and, as often happens, he is not able to tolerate success. His inability to be a success could then be traced to guilt arising from castration complex etc. It could be revealed to him, and he could be suitably reconciled and adjusted to his lot.
>
> On the other hand one might say, that he is indeed suffering from guilt—but not guilt which is the punishment of the ego by the super-ego, but guilt which arises when a man neglects or ignores or denies his own true, authentic possibilities, and refuses to see what is happening. Such a view is not mutually exclusive of the first, but there is nothing in the first (orthodox Freudian) to point to the second. (Mullan, 1997, p. 78)

The preceding example concerns an individual case. But Laing also managed an elegant synthesis of existential and analytic perspectives in his handling of group therapy in chapter 8 of *Self and Others*. Following Buber, Laing noted that all people desire confirmation from others, but that in the absence of real trust and self-confidence, genuine self-disclosure is impossible. The absence of genuine self-disclosure and mutual confirmation, in turn, prompts people who are hungry for some form of relatedness to settle for "counterfeits," which are based on the complementarity of one another's *false* selves or imaginary identities—a *shared* pretence sustained by tacit agreement and intricately intertwined with what Laing termed *collusion*.

To illustrate this point, Laing discussed an all-male therapy group consisting of seven members ages twenty-five to thirty-five. With one exception—"Bill"—they were all reasonably successful, middle-class patients. (Bill lived at home and was between jobs.) At first, the group tried putting Laing in the position of "the one who knows" or who has the answer to their various problems. When these efforts failed, one member, "Jack," took the leadership role upon himself, attempting to "help" the various participants talk about their problems in living, and in so doing, presumably, help their therapist help *them* more effectively, if and when the therapist chose to do so.

While most group members were grateful for Jack's initiative, Bill soon developed a homosexual "crush" on him. While he did not confess it openly, his feelings became apparent to the others, who expressed their fear and revulsion obliquely by vigorous assertions of their masculinity and by a collective denial of homosexual feelings through ritualistic "male bonding" behavior. Their need to reciprocally and repeatedly affirm their heterosexuality suggested a strong need to deny diffuse sexual tensions within the group—or so Laing thought.

What made this scenario intriguing, however, was that prior to alluding furtively to his crush on Jack, Bill had had a close collusive relationship with him, one that confirmed Jack's informal status as a distinctively generous and helpful group leader in exchange for Jack's confirming Bill's image of himself as a cultured, sensitive, and uniquely misunderstood and unlucky individual. Both derived obvious pleasure from this arrangement, and their dialogue along these lines was the chief focus of discussion in the initial phases of the group's existence. When this handy collusive "engine" for nullifying silence and collective anxiety was hastily abandoned, another was promptly contrived, this one fueled by strategies of denial of any homosexual inclinations. Now, Laing observed, the cordial partnership between (active) Jack and (passive) Bill degenerated into a sadomasochistic dialogue in which, for example, Jack attacked Bill for not enjoying football matches, prompting Bill to cringe in pain and horror.

One could construe the group processes just described in Freudian terms, as the result of the simultaneous repression/denial of homosexual components in all six psyches, repression and denial being "defense mechanisms" mobilized by an individual's "ego" to obstruct objectionable "component instincts" from entering consciousness. Laing found this language cumbersome and arcane. Collusion, as Laing conceived it, is not an individual or intrapsychic process but an interpersonal (that is, *social*) event, albeit one with little social visibility. Collusion in Laing's sense is an unspoken bargain struck simultaneously with oneself and with others—a bargain whose existence is ignored or denied by those party to it. Partners in a collusive relationship need not seek the same practical objectives and may act for very different motives, depending on circumstances. But ultimately, all that is required to sustain a collusive relationship is that their objectives *are not in conflict with one another*, and that those party to the bargain are oblivious to it, even if it is transparent to outsiders. Once group processes have been framed in these terms, there is no need to invoke competing or conflicting agencies *within the psyche* of this or that particular person to explain or describe what transpired. Nor need one invoke the theory of infantile sexuality, the Oedipus complex, and so on.[2]

Nevertheless, at this point, Laing's interpretation of group processes had an obviously Freudian inflection. As Laing experienced things unfolding in the group, homosexual tensions percolated slowly to the surface then were vigorously disavowed, though their collective denial merely confirmed their underlying existence. And on a somewhat Lacanian note, Laing noted, the analyst was supposed to "have the answer," be the "one who knows," yet he steadfastly refused that position. In his own words:

> A large part of the art of therapy is in the tact and lucidity with which the analyst points out the ways in which collusion maintains illusions or disguises delusions. The dominant phantasy in a group may be that the therapist has "the answer," and if they had "the answer" they would not suffer. The therapist's task is then like the Zen master's, to point out that suffering is not due to not getting "the answer," but is the very state of desire that assumes the existence of that kind of answer, and the frustration of never getting it. (1961, pp. 123–124)

In view of the Freudian and Lacanian inflections one detects here, it is also instructive to note the things that Laing did *not* say. Unlike a classical Freudian, he did not claim that *all* male groups reenact the conflicts of the "primal horde" or are bound together by sublimated homoerotic tendencies and a shared idealization/hatred of the group "leader." Nor did he say that Bill's crush on Jack—and in due course, on his analyst—was a transference of his feelings toward his father, and therefore symptomatic of an inadequate resolution to his Oedipal (and/or reverse-Oedipal) conflicts. Unlike a Lacanian, Laing did not construe Bill's longing for passive homosexual contact with his analyst as evidence that the father's phallus is the "true" object of unconscious desire, or as proof of his ostensible inability to enter the symbolic order. Nor did he assert that the phantasy of the analyst as the "one who knows" is the central or invariant theme of patients' (conscious or unconscious) imaginings. Claims and generalizations of this order go far beyond the actual data and violate Laing's phenomenologically rooted insistence on vivid description accompanied by cautious interpretation.

In any case, if there is one clear therapeutic directive to be extracted from *Self and Others,* it is that the therapist must patiently attempt to elucidate the ways in which the patient is involved in and/or victimized by collusive relationships with others. The same would presumably apply for the other interpersonal processes that Laing describes so vividly: double binds (Bateson), false and untenable positions, attributions and injunctions, and so on. Since Laing's clinical vignettes usually describe contemporaneous events and processes rather than childhood recollections, the tacit implication is that understanding the present is as important as understanding the past—a recurrent theme in the literature on existential therapy (Cohn, 1994). The deeper subtext is that individual phantasy is less the reflection of conflicted instincts or agencies within the psyche than of defective patterns of relatedness and communication within the interpersonal world in which the psyche is embedded.

This is very useful, and on the face of it, perhaps, compatible with *The Divided Self.* But again, remember that the previous book contrasted the schizoid fear of self-disclosure and relatedness with the robust benefits of ontological security, which confers an ability for genuine self-disclosure and autonomous relatedness to others. Thus there was a measure of optimism in the message conveyed by

The Divided Self—that fears of self-disclosure, and of engulfment, petrification, implosion, and so on, can be dispelled and the capacity for relatedness restored.

But in *Self and Others,* Laing apparently lost some of his therapeutic optimism. He no longer defined normality as a state of ontological security, but as a state of unconscious complicity in "collective phantasy systems"—which I will explain more fully elsewhere. Those who inhabit a "tenable position" in a collective phantasy system seem to thrive, to be "in touch with reality." But by virtue of their shared estrangement from existential actualities, they are actually incapable of experiencing, expressing, or sharing much of anything genuine with one another, though they are perforce unaware of their condition (pp. 40–41). The upshot of this line of thinking, which is articulated more forcefully in *The Politics of Experience,* is that direct, unmediated I-Thou relationships—or core-to-core relatedness, as Erich Fromm called it—is all but impossible now. In the present circumstances, all that can reasonably be hoped for are fleeting intimations of what genuine relatedness *would* be like, if only . . .

So, while enjoining tact, lucidity, and hermeneutic continence on the part of the therapist, Laing's second book, *Self and Others,* sounded a soft, despairing note that builds to a furious crescendo in *The Politics of Experience.* What makes this contrast more curious, in retrospect, is that *The Divided Self* and *Self and Others,* published one year apart, were actually *written* concurrently and originally intended as part of a three-volume series. (Volume 3 never materialized.)

Judging from this and other data, it seems that rapid and mysterious oscillations between optimistic and pessimistic views of the human condition were woven into the whole fabric of Laing's thought and character. For example, take *Interpersonal Perception,* published in 1966, which Laing thought of as a belated sequel to *Self and Others.* It focused on the remediation of marital conflict and was decidedly *upbeat* about the prospects for couples in which both spouses, no matter how angry and estranged from one another, are essentially honest with themselves, capable of empathizing accurately with another person's point of view, and patient enough to unravel the multiple misunderstandings that gave rise to recurrent tensions.

But *Interpersonal Perception* (1966) was followed immediately by *The Politics of Experience* (1967), and after that, by *The Politics of the Family* (1969), which were both profoundly pessimistic books. *Knots* (1970), by contrast, was more detached, though leaning toward a retreat from the concerns of a practicing therapist to a realm of Platonic ideas (Burston, 1996a). *The Facts of Life* (1976) was widely viewed as another pessimistic offering; see, for example, Anthony Storr's review (1977), which was fairly representative. But Laing insisted publicly that this book was more optimistic than anything he had written in a very long time (Itten in Mullan, 1997).

In 1980, Douglas Kirsner interviewed Laing at home and asked him about optimism, pessimism, and the human condition. Laing replied flippantly that he was "an optimist on Mondays, Thursdays and Saturdays, and a pessimist on Wednesdays and Sundays." On a serious note, he added that his philosophical position justified neither optimism nor pessimism, which in the final analysis are merely moods. Moods do not prove anything, nor can they be proven by anything, since any amount of information can be "fed" into these states of mind with apparently plausible results.

Kirsner then asked Laing about alienation and estrangement in the contemporary world and the prospect for genuine human relationships. Laing responded in effect that while he made ample allowance for the elements of tragedy and contingency that pervade human existence, he took issue with Freud's contention that in contemporary life simple, natural human love is impossible. Laing felt quite comfortable with many features of contemporary society, which are a vast improvement on many things a mere century before (Laing with Kirsner in Mullan, 1997).

With all due respect, we must not take Laing at face value here. His first reply, while intended for comic effect, was actually quite revealing. It suggests a regular (though mysterious) alternation between optimism and pessimism, though judging by the number of days accorded to each—three for optimism, two for pessimism, and two unaccounted for—Kirsner found Laing in a predominantly *optimistic* frame of mind. Second, in construing optimism and pessimism as moods that are extraneous to substantive philosophy, Laing echoed Heidegger, who dismissed discussion of his own work in these terms as utterly vacuous. But whatever its source or rationale, this emphatic disclaimer just does not tally with the subtle but profound disparities between *The Divided Self*

(1960) and *Self and Others* (1961), or the very dramatic differences evidenced in *The Politics of Experience* (1967), *Interpersonal Perception* (1996), and other works.

In fairness to Laing, there are many aspects of his work that do elude understanding purely in terms of these "moods"—though I prefer to call them attitudes. Indeed, if one were looking for common denominators or overarching ideas, one could trace the invariant themes that suffuse his work. In fact, that is largely what this book is intended to achieve. But even so, there is no doubt that these opposed "moods" gripped Laing dramatically, and often unpredictably, and that he was either unable or unwilling to reflect on and account for them in his work. Instead, to judge by the evidence, he simply wrote as the spirit moved him.

Of all his books, *The Divided Self* is the source of Laing's most engaging reflections on existential psychotherapy. Though it does not prescribe specific techniques, it gives a clear indication of his therapeutic goals and a vivid idea of how he went about achieving them with very disturbed patients. For that very reason, however, it is sometimes difficult to decide to what extent his later works are consonant or contiguous with his initial offering. This is not a problem when comparing *The Divided Self* with *Self and Others,* since despite subtle shifts on the prospects for relatedness, they share an obvious concern with the issues of self-deception and pretence, and with enabling patients to assume responsibility for themselves. Similarly, there are strong threads of continuity between *Self and Others* and *Interpersonal Perception,* on the one hand, and *The Politics of Experience,* on the other.

One of the first breaks in Laing's conceptual continuity emerges when we get to Laing's "rebirthing" phase. For despite his early and intriguing reference to traumatic birth as a factor in Julie's case, there is a profound disparity between Laing's ideas on "existential birth" circa 1960 and his ideas on the origins of self-consciousness (and memory) a decade later. In *The Divided Self,* Laing maintained that existential birth is a process that follows at some unspecified time soon after birth, when the infant's awareness of being the object of another person's intentional activities, of being an entity *for the other* (one addressed by the other, and so forth) catalyzes the emergence of being *for oneself,* or self-consciousness. At this point, Laing was developing and deepening Hegelian, Sartrean, and Buberian tropes on the nature and origins of human subjectivity.

But a decade later, in *The Facts of Life* (1976), Laing attributed a dim awareness of the mother's attitude and intentions to a zygote prior to implantation in the uterine wall, some eight months before a normal birth. This is not merely a shift in emphasis: it is a dramatically different claim. Moreover, Laing suggested that the self/world schemata acquired *prior* to birth have a more formative and lingering influence on the domain of "unconscious phantasy," and by implication, the whole domain of human feelings, than events occurring postpartum—at least in many middle-aged adults.

In fairness to Laing, trying to periodize the emergence of human self-consciousness with any degree of precision is still fraught with considerable risk—even now, when infant research is vastly more sophisticated than it was at mid-century. Today it is apparent to all that there is much more continuity between prenatal and postnatal life than anyone imagined in 1960 (e.g., Stern, 1985). But if history is any guide, then as we probe deeper into the mysteries of the mind, we will probably be obliged to revise repeatedly our timetables for the dawning of self-awareness. So the mere fact that Laing revised his thinking is not the issue. The problem is that he failed to acknowledge the ramifications—indeed, the very existence—of this shift. Had Laing been more attentive, and more concerned with establishing continuity and consistency in his work, he might have explained this development in more detail. As it is, he never did, and we can only surmise that he was either oblivious to these facts or willfully preferred to ignore them.

In any case, if we set aside Laing's conjectures about intrauterine experience and focus solely on the work that preceded it, we are left with the following distillation of his views, which applies widely to the treatment of patients. According to Laing, the goals of individual psychotherapy are

1. to restore the person's capacity for relatedness to others and authentic self-disclosure,
2. to reduce anxiety by overcoming the person's feelings/fears of engulfment, implosion, and petrification,
3. to help patients to differentiate between "true" and "false" guilt, and to minimize or abolish the latter, and
4. to make the "unconscious" conscious, not in classical Freudian fashion, but by both illuminating the person's recourse to pretence and self-deception, at the personal level, and elucidating

patterns of collusion and/or mystification they are enmeshed in, at the interpersonal and/or the institutional level.

If these are the *goals* of therapy, how are they achieved? On reflection, most of Laing's "treatment recommendations" are framed negatively, in terms of what the therapist ought to *avoid*. One hesitates to use the term "method" here, though it is clearly preferable to "technique." For lack of a better word, we will summarize Laing's approach as follows. On a positive note, Laing recommends that during the therapeutic interview, therapists

1. express tact, courtesy, and empathy for patients, and
2. be fully awake, aware, and present to them.

Negatively, he recommended that therapists

3. not be judgmental,
4. not attempt to fit the patient's utterances or experiences into a preconceived diagnostic or theoretical schema,
5. not engage in excessive interpretation/conjecture, that is, stick close to the data at hand (hermeneutic restraint), and
6. not collude with the patients fantasies, or their efforts to create or maintain false identities.

Finally, there is a seventh therapeutic injunction that I have not broached so far, but which I address toward the end of Chapter 4, namely

7. get the "family," that is, family myths, out of one's system.

* * *

Having distilled the essence of Laing's approach to psychotherapy, I conclude this chapter with some reflections on hitherto unacknowledged tensions in Laing's concepts of therapeutic agency and change, and the role of interpretation in therapy. These are offered in a spirit of charitable skepticism and without reproach. Most of the contradictions noted below are rather slight, and may be more apparent than real in some cases. Besides, as any experienced therapist knows, perfect congruence between theory and practice is difficult to achieve, and conceptual contradictions—especially ones that are not formulated or even conscious—can be a fertile source of deeper insight once they have been brought to light.

Though Laing never discussed it explicitly, there is a tension between the Buberian and Heideggerian philosophies that has implications for the practice of individual psychotherapy. Buber noted that to truly know someone presupposes the existence of an I-Thou relationship. One can know a great deal *about* someone without really knowing him or her. Accumulating facts about an individual's medical, family, ethnic, and educational background and making inferences from these facts on the basis of previous experience—all of this, while legitimate and arguably indispensable to therapy, can be conducted competently within the detached and depersonalized I-It mode. Similarly, one can *speak* to another as the bearer or embodiment of all of these real or hypothetical qualities, totalized in various ways, and yet in a deeper sense not address him or her at all—"communication without communion," as Laing put it (1985, p. 40).

No matter how expert or well intentioned the therapist, activities or interventions within the I-It framework give us little leverage in the long run. The real agent of change and transformation lies in the therapist being fully present to the other and affirming the patient's existence through their interactions. This in itself is therapeutic and apt to foster greater openness and awareness. Only then can one invoke and address the other in his or her full humanity. At the same time, as noted previously, the prophetic sensibility in Buber allows for candid confrontation in an I-Thou relationship. Indeed, it calls for it explicitly. In short, communion must precede confrontation, or it will fail. But communion absent confrontation will ultimately lapse into sterility and pointlessness.

Contrast this with the Heideggerian approach. Heidegger's friend and pupil, Medard Boss, commended Heidegger for capturing in *Being and Time* the essence of the therapeutic posture in the distinction between different modes of care or solicitude: "einspringende Fürsorge" and "vorspringende Fürsorge". The former, explained Heidegger, is active and intrusive. Like medical treatment, it makes a deliberate project out of changing the patient in certain specific ways, in conformity with a preconceived concept of health. The latter, by contrast, respects the dignity and uniqueness of the person. It "lets Being be," as Heidegger said, and thereby enables the person to bring his or her own potential for being into fruition.

In some ways, Heidegger's distinction between "einspringende Fürsorge" and "vorspringende Fürsorge" echoes Buber's distinction between I-It and I-Thou relationships. Accordingly, one might suppose that the area of convergence between Buber and Boss is far greater than the scope of their differences. Perhaps it is. After all, Buber and Boss shared the goals of restoring openness to others and underlined the necessity of accepting and affirming the patient and eschewing a detached professional posture. And like Laing a little later, they both emphasized that change and transformation spring from the quality of relatedness between therapist and patient, rather than from following a correct "technique."

Nevertheless, judging from their language, Buber's approach is emphatically more *agentic*. Buber used the term "meeting" as a verb—implying an attitude of active engagement—not as a noun to describe a particular kind of event. By contrast, Boss, following Heidegger, adopted a stance that is exquisitely *receptive* and subtly mistrustful of human agency, as evidenced by Heidegger's "Will not to will" and his writings on technology.[3]

Taken to extremes, of course, each approach is liable to exaggeration. Buber's prophetic sensibility could be mistaken for mere moralism, or as an instance of "einspringende Fürsorge," which makes change in the patient a deliberate project, a demand. Conversely, Boss's reflections on therapeutic openness could be caricatured as a variant of Rogers's "unconditional positive regard," which places no conditions or demands whatsoever on the patient.

It is not my intention to ratify or dismiss either view, or to ascertain how much of their apparent difference is due to a mere difference in emphasis, inflection and/or mutual misunderstanding. As important as these questions are for existential psychotherapists, the point I am making is that both of these "voices" or perspectives can readily be found in Laing. For example, in *The Politics of Experience,* chapter 2, entitled "The Psychotherapeutic Experience," Laing writes: "Any technique concerned with . . . an object-to-be-changed rather than a person to be accepted simply perpetuates the disease it purports to cure" (p. 53). This is an essentially Heideggerian view. But a few pages later, in *The Bird of Paradise,* Laing muses, "If I could turn you on, if I could drive you out of your wretched mind, if I could tell you, I would let you know" (p. 185). Here Laing's tone is deeply, even bitterly, confrontational.

Judging from these remarks, and from conversations with Laing's patients and supervisees, the different therapeutic postures mandated by Buber and Heidegger respectively were *both* endorsed by Laing, and were applied as needed in different contexts. The more disturbed the patient—and the more disturbing to others—the more often and intently Laing took a Heideggerian approach, emphasizing unqualified acceptance as the sine qua non of therapeutic effectiveness. The less disturbed, the more "normal" the patient, the more Buberian he was apt to be. Laing never addressed this issue in writing, and so never encountered any commentary or criticism on this score, at least to my knowledge. But the question then emerges: despite its philosophic justification—or rather, the lack of it—was this tacit shift in position useful or justified? (Evidently Laing thought so, though he never had occasion to actually say so, much less to explain why.)

A similar ambiguity surrounds the role of interpretation in psychotherapy. For the most part, when talking with patients, Laing eschewed overt interpretations. Yet many therapists with whom I spoke—and I spoke mostly with American psychiatrists who had worked with Laing for a year or more—said that at case conferences and in clinical supervision, Laing had an uncanny knack for formulating their patients' issues in conventional analytic terminology. Several found his formulations so incisive that when his supervision ended they felt as if they had been "introduced" to their patients for the first time—that is, they saw them in a dramatically new light that changed the direction of their work irrevocably and for the better. Others reported that his appraisals seemed tenuous or opaque at first, but made abundant sense later on, as the therapy progressed. No one I spoke to expressed disappointment or dismay about his style of supervision, though a few said that despite appearances and his flaming, radical rhetoric, Laing was really an astute but remarkably conventional analyst—or could function that way if circumstances required.

My favorite anecdote along these lines comes from Morton Schatzman, who was relating his experiences with a patient to Laing sometime in 1968. After several minutes, in an effort to relax and concentrate, he said, Laing stood on his head in a Yogic posture while Schatzman talked on for the remainder of the session. As the supervisory session was drawing to a close, Laing, who had been silent thus far, delivered a rich, concise, and insightful analysis of the case in about three minutes and declared the session over. He was still standing on his head when Schatzman left.

These stories are striking in that none of Laing's peers or supervisees felt that his way of formulating cases in conventional analytic language did violence to their (or their patients') experience or detracted from their understanding of their patients as people. So while Laing was consistent on the need for hermeneutic restraint on the therapist's part, he evidently felt that such restrictions are not binding on the therapist's *supervisor*. Given that Laing was so prescient and insightful in formulating other people's cases, one can only suppose that he was also capable of thinking about his own patients' utterances and experiences in ways that were disjunctive with his own approach to existential dialogue, which emphasized empathy and *Verstehen*, but for the most part proscribed interpretation.

Evidence for this line of conjecture, though somewhat scarce, is not impossible to find. For example, Leon Redler recalls a conversation with Laing in 1970, in which he, Redler, proposed to invite a Zen Buddhist master to become more closely involved in the affairs of the Philadelphia Association. To Redler's surprise, Laing objected that "those guys"—that is, meditation instructors, gurus, and so on—"don't analyze the transference." As Redler recalls, this remark took him aback, as Laing himself never "analyzed the transference." Or not in so many words. But the implication of Laing's remark was that, in his own mind, he *was* analyzing the transference and shaping his responses to patients accordingly, even if he did not *interpret* the transference overtly.

One more feature of Laing's approach that warrants discussion but is not mentioned in his published work is the issue of *memory*. Jan Resnick, who worked with Laing for ten years, recalls being profoundly moved by his brilliant recall, often verbatim, of lengthy conversations from sessions they had done months previously. Other patients reported similar experiences. Laing always insisted that empathy and attentiveness are the proverbial bottom line. But being fully present to the patient, here and now, does not mean forgetting what transpired before. The ability to recall what the patient said ten weeks (or months) previously about a topic of potential importance enables the patient to ponder subtle but sometimes important shifts in his or her feelings, attitudes, and own selective recall of relatively recent events. It fosters more patient and thoughtful introspection on the patient's part, and sends him or her the powerful message that the therapist values the patient highly enough to remember what was said. In short, the therapist deploys memory in the attempt to "mirror" the patient's existence faithfully, rather than to gloat over apparent inconsistencies.

FAMILIES, PHENOMENOLOGY, AND SCHIZOPHRENIA

··· 4 ···

Thus far we have looked at Laing's views on individual and group psychotherapy. But what of family therapy? Laing was well known as a family theorist, yet oddly enough never wrote a single word about the *practice* of family therapy. To compound the mystery, his friendships with pioneers in this field—Don Jackson, Ray Birdwhistell, Lyman Wynne, Ross Speck, Jay Haley, Paul Watzlawick, Virginia Satir, and Salvador Minuchin—are a matter of record. Indeed, a curious feature of Laing's career is that as his reputation declined during the seventies and eighties, many family therapists still held him in considerable esteem. This is doubly odd because his approach was diametrically *opposed* to theirs in crucial respects. For example, family therapists typically foster therapeutic alliances between a clinician and the parents in the family. Laing, by contrast, often questioned such alliances and aligned himself with the children instead.

When Richard Simon (1983) drew attention to this approach in an interview for the *Family Therapy Networker,* Laing replied brusquely that children can drive their parents mad just as surely and effectively as the other way around, and that he regretted never having said so before. To the best of my knowledge, this is the only published acknowledgment he gave of his one-sidedness in this regard. (For more on this point, see Fort, 1990.) When Simon then asked why Laing never wrote about his own approach to family treatment, his response was that he did not want *other* therapists to make their careers by peddling diluted and distorted versions of his ideas—particularly in socialist or social democratic countries, where family therapy might be compulsory and where failure to follow a therapist's directives could lead to state-enforced sanctions.

In truth, Laing's reticence on the practice of family therapy was probably due more to his complicated personal history as a theorist, therapist, and family man, which is not at issue here. Still, one reason he was so vehement on this point is that he was frequently associated with leftist critiques of the family—an association he deplored increasingly as he grew older.[1] For example, as recently as 1980, in a book entitled *Critical Theory of the Family,* Laing was commended for offering a radical alternative to both psychoanalytically oriented approaches (such as those offered by Nathan Ackerman and Theodor Lidz) and the more recent (and more popular) structural and systemic methods. The author, Mark Poster, said that despite different emphases, these approaches all foster conformity and the maintenance of the status quo at the expense of genuine autonomy and sociability. Laing's approach, though too mystical for his taste, offered a viable way out of the family straitjacket (Poster, 1980, ch. 5).

Poster's appraisal was fairly representative. Though Laing never referred to him by name, Poster's remarks might been more palatable had he not linked Laing with his erstwhile colleague David Cooper. In fairness to Poster, and others like him, he is not to blame for making this linkage. Laing and Cooper had joined forces to found the Philadelphia Association (in 1963), to co-author a book (in 1964), to create various therapeutic communities (in 1965 and 1966), to convene The Dialectics of Liberation Conference (in 1967), and to help a group of activists found London's "Anti-University" (in 1968). Evidently, Poster did not know that Cooper's book *The Death of the Family* (1971), which Laing detested, was the last straw in a relationship that had been seriously strained since the autumn of 1967, when Laing, who was already somewhat disenchanted with the Left, took offense at being labeled an "antipsychiatrist" by Cooper (Mullan, 1995).

By his own admission, Laing never dissociated himself from Cooper vigorously enough to make an impression on the educated public (Mullan, 1995). As a result, the lines of cleavage between Cooper and Laing were crystal clear to him, but extremely murky to others. And with good reason. Look at Laing's flaming best-seller, *The Politics of Experience*, published in 1967. Laing talked about families in two sections of this book. Chapter 3, entitled "The Mystification of Experience," was the chief source of difficulty. Here he likened the family to a "mutual protection racket," charging that its real function is "to repress Eros; to induce a false consciousness of security; to deny death by avoiding life; to cut off transcendence . . . to promote respect, conformity, obedience . . . (and) respect for 'respectability'" (p. 55).

In addition, Laing attacked Theodor Lidz, who saw the primary function of the family as facilitating the process of adaptation. "Adaptation to what?" asked Laing indignantly. "To society? To a world gone mad?"

As I noted previously in *The Wing of Madness*, Laing made a valid point by questioning the claims to value neurality made by Lidz and others. You cannot be *for* adaptation to prevailing social norms and claim to be neutral at the same time. Disavowing your bias, or pretending it isn't a bias, is not science but rather scientism and pseudo-objectivity. Yet Laing's antinomian view of adaptation (in which we trade security and pseudo-sanity for authenticity), while less disingenuous, is also problematic. As we see in Chapter 5, inverting commonsense assumptions about the nature of normality is a potentially useful and illuminating procedure. But if the resulting insights assume the character of inflated and dogmatically held generalizations, they are apt to be equally misleading.

Despite all the rhetoric of yesterday's pundits, adaptation per se is neither good nor bad. From a Darwinian standpoint, needless to say, it is a purely *neutral* and amoral process. It is not "progressive" or "positive"; it just is what it is. From an ethical and/or psychological standpoint, adaptation is also a neutral or at most ambiguous category or trait, denoting psychic processes that may enhance or diminish our humanity, depending on circumstances. Before we can determine whether adaptation is good or bad for our mental health, we must always specify what we are adapting to, and how we are adapting to it. Then, and only then, is meaningful discussion possible.

Though profound, provocative, and illuminating in many ways, *The Politics of Experience* suffered somewhat from the kind of bombastic excess that says adaptation per se is detrimental to the human spirit. By standing conventional prejudices on their head, it denied itself a sure and credible footing. Fortunately, chapter 5, entitled "The Schizophrenic Experience," was a little less polemical and a lot more pertinent to our purposes. Here Laing gave readers a brief overview of research on the families of schizophrenics, a summation that emphasized his affinities with Erving Goffman and Gregory Bateson. The key similarity, he said, is a strategic shift away from traditional attempts to pinpoint the locus of "pathology" within the brain or the unconscious of the identified patient, toward seeing the patient's psychological disturbance (and its neurophysiological correlates) as symptomatic of disturbances within the family— disturbances that place the identified patient in an "unlivable" or "checkmate" situation that he cannot elucidate, tolerate, or change. Accordingly, "the behavior of the diagnosed patient is part of a much larger network of disturbed behavior. The contradictions and confusions 'internalized' by the individual must be looked at in their larger social contexts" (p. 96).

Laing hastened to add that discovering the source of a patient's difficulties is not a matter of laying blame. After all, they are seldom a matter of conscious manipulation or dishonesty—although such deceit is much more common than is generally supposed. More often than not, the unlivable situation that provokes a patient's breakdown is "by definition *not obvious* to the protagonists." Sadly enough, it is equally obscure to the psychiatrists who are called upon to intervene.

Viewed phenomenologically, said Laing, a patient's bizarre ideas and utterances are often intelligible responses to the complex and contradictory messages, demands, and prescriptions imposed on them by others. By the same token, however, a patient's family often has a shared interest in *not* seeing a symptom's meaning or function, by invalidating the experience and behavior of the patient, by construing it as deranged, depraved, and so on. Indeed, the average psychiatrist lacks the requisite experience or motivation to see through these collective machinations and denials and generally colludes with the family, thereby becoming part of the "conspiracy."

To illustrate what Laing was saying here, let us cast our minds back to chapter 9 of *The Divided Self*. There we find a brief vignette about a hitherto "normal" man in his fifties whom, for sake of convenience, I will call Henry. One summer afternoon, Henry went picnicking with his wife and children. After the meal, in full view of passersby, Henry stripped naked, waded into the nearby river, and doused himself repeatedly, saying he was baptizing himself for his sins. When asked *what* sins, Henry declared that he had never really loved his wife and children. Moreover, he refused to come out of the river until he was "cleansed." He was eventually dragged out by the police and hospitalized immediately thereafter (p. 148).

Admittedly, Henry was behaving in an odd, tactless, and obstinate manner. But why is the presumption in such circumstances that he was losing his mind, rather than finding it? And why do we invariably suspect that there is something wrong with Henry's brain, rather than a tumult in his soul? Even if his guilt feelings are "delusional," in some sense, why do most of us write him off before we even ponder the nature of his alleged transgressions? Was he guilty of deceiving himself or others, or was lovelessness his deepest sin? Having probed that point, we might then ask ourselves *whom* he had sinned against (in his own mind, anyway)—his family, himself, his God, or all three?

Though the baptismal symbolism is transparent, Henry's intention of atoning for his (real or imagined) sins by dousing himself repeatedly was silly, desperate, and perhaps a little histrionic. Even so, his claim that he never really loved his wife and children, rather than being delusional, just might be true. As catastrophic as this realization may be for all concerned, it is better to acknowledge a bitter truth and cope with its consequences than to live a lie—or so Henry felt, apparently.

The odds are that his wife felt otherwise, however. Indeed, she probably was horrified at this disclosure and felt that this raving fool was not the man she married. Any effort to uncover the real truth of the matter, by patiently sifting fact from fantasy, truth from fiction, all the way back to their courtship (and perhaps, if necessary, beyond), would inevitably expose Henry's wife to raw feelings of anger, inadequacy, shame, and betrayal as she got to know the man behind the mask—arguably for the very first time. Even if she were up to the challenge, there is no guarantee that Henry would ever be restored to health—or more precisely, to his "pre-morbid condition"—which may be what she would prefer. So psychotherapy is a dubious proposition for all concerned. Evidently, from a psychiatric standpoint, some somatic intervention is called for to put poor Henry in his "right" mind again.

Laing does not inform us what Henry's diagnosis was. But when this event took place—circa 1955, I am guessing—Henry, in the

United Kingdom, was only half as likely to be diagnosed as schizophrenic than if he were in the United States. The striking contrast between overzealous Americans and their more cautious British and European counterparts generated much controversy in the ensuing decades, most of it focused on how quickly or carefully clinicians diagnose, and what criteria they use to determine the nature of a patient's "illness." Few doubted that patients like Henry actually suffered from a *medical* illness, however, even though they had no "hard" evidence to support this conjecture. In any event, in view of where he lived and was treated, Henry was probably diagnosed as a case of agitated depression with psychotic features, and received insulin or electroshock treatment combined with antidepressant drugs. Had Henry waded in American waters, the outcome would have been different. He would probably have been diagnosed as schizophrenic and treated accordingly. How reliable would this diagnosis have been, and what kind of treatment would he have received?

Oddly enough, in the 1950s, American psychiatrists were aware of the disparity between themselves and their Continental cousins, but were not troubled by the fact that they used the diagnosis "schizophrenia" twice as often, on average. The situation began to change around 1973, when David Rosenhan, an American psychologist, published "On Being Sane in Insane Places" in *Science,* an article known in the mental health professions as the "pseudopatient" study.

Dr. Rosenhan instructed eight of his students and colleagues to feign an auditory hallucination just long enough to gain admittance to a local mental hospital. Once there, they dropped any pretence of being mad and kept careful records of daily events and their thoughts, feelings, and experiences. Their stays on the wards varied from seven to fifty-two days, because in some instances they had difficulty convincing the doctors and staff that they were normal and had to get outside help to extricate themselves from the hospital. Why? Their claims that they were researchers participating in a study were treated as delusional, and their note-taking was dismissed as typically paranoid behavior. Indeed, noted Rosenhan wryly, the inmates on the wards detected the normality of his researchers long before the staff did. In fact, to be perfectly truthful, the doctors and nurses involved never did recognize their normality. Without exception, when they left the hospital, Rosenhan's accomplices were given the diagnosis of "schizophrenia in remission."

Rosenhan's study generated tremendous controversy because it implied that psychiatrists cannot reliably discriminate between the sane and the mad, and that the treatment afforded to people diagnosed as schizophrenic is likely to aggravate rather than alleviate their condition, whatever it may be. As Rosenhan made clear, there is nothing "therapeutic" about the average mental hospital. While on the wards, Rosenhan's researchers all experienced feelings of profound boredom, powerlessness, and depersonalization. And they all reported what Laing (and others) had called attention to—the absence of real solidarity, of any meaningful communication, between the hospital staff and inmates. One anecdote from Rosenhan's study concerns a nurse who unself-consciously opened her blouse to adjust her bra in full view of a whole ward of male patients. This gesture was not intended seductively, or even as a provocation. Rather, she behaved as if these patients were simply not there.

Another troubling aspect of Rosenhan's study was the way in which the "pseudo-patients" were experienced and, in due course, discharged by hospital staff. Once they had been labeled schizophrenic, anything Rosenhan's colleagues said or did counted as evidence confirming or merely modifying the initial diagnosis, rather than reversing or disconfirming it. Clearly, the doctors and nurses involved could not admit their errors, and preferred to punish Rosenhan's confederates with the stigma of "schizophrenia in remission" rather than acknowledge the truth and their own fallibility.

As disturbing and provocative as Rosenhan's study was, there was one thing he did not question—namely, the actual *existence* of schizophrenia as a diagnosable disease. Laing did, however (Laing, 1967). And though Laing may be proven wrong eventually, one must admire the courage and clarity he mustered in defiance of the prevailing consensus. Even today, after more than a century of speculation and research, a clear-cut and convincing etiology for schizophrenia is still lacking. And though psychiatrists—and many historians, anthropologists, and others—concur that schizophrenia has afflicted humanity since time immemorial (such as Rosen, 1968), there are no references to this elusive entity in the work of early psychiatrists like Phillipe Pinel, Jean Esquirol, Benjamin Rush, or

Wilhelm Greisinger. In short, *nothing* until the middle of the nineteenth century.

There is plenty of evidence, however, that people deemed mad had hallucinations and delusions and were weird, silly, obstinate, revolting, and sometimes dangerous to themselves or others. And if one is so inclined, one can interpret their behavior in light of contemporary categories. Even for historians, who should know better, the temptation to do so is often irresistible. But as Laing points out, the first reference to anything like schizophrenia was in 1860, when Belgian psychiatrist Benedict-Augustin Morel was consulted by a distressed father (and family friend) about his fourteen-year-old son. "Antoine" was an exceptional young scholar who, according to his father, had suddenly expressed a violent aversion toward him, which included thoughts of parricide. The father said that Antoine's anger was completely unprecedented—that prior to this point, Antoine had only shown a deep and affectionate regard for him.

Because Antoine was short for his age, because his mother was hospitalized for insanity, and because his maternal grandmother was quite eccentric, Morel suspected some combination of hereditary insanity and "arrest in development." Accordingly, he had Antoine confined to a sanatorium for observation and treatment, which included gymnastic exercises, manual labor, and baths. Ironically, Antoine grew in stature but became duller and less communicative in Morel's care. Indeed, after a year of treatment, he seemed to forget everything he had learned and entered a state of "torpor" in which he stopped speaking altogether. Morel concluded that a premature dementia, or *demence precocé,* had brought this precocious child's development to a tragic halt (1860). Similar cases, from Morel and others, followed, and in 1899, Morel's term was Latinized by Emile Kraepelin as *dementia praecox.*

Laing cited Morel in *The Politics of the Family,* though only for purposes of deconstruction (Laing, 1972, pp. 70–72). According to Laing, Morel aligned himself with the father and assumed that Antoine's hatred really was sudden, unprecedented, and unjustified. He made no effort to determine the boy's side of the story. But what if Antoine's hatred was justified, Laing asked? What if his father was a clever scoundrel who hospitalized his mother to silence or punish her—which was ridiculously easy in those days, as John Stuart Mill and Elizabeth Packard attested (Mill, 1858; Packard,

1873)? If so, then the diagnosis of hereditary insanity (along the maternal line) would merely disguise the oppression of the mother and her child, in which the psychiatrist was an unwitting (but thoroughly obliging) accomplice (Laing, 1970, pp. 69–75).[2]

Some dismiss this argument as paranoid. Why distrust a poor father's testimony? Yet Laing had spent more than a decade researching schizophrenia and discovered that patient's "delusions" often contain much truth, literal and figurative. Moreover, according to Laing, collusions between psychiatrists and hateful parents or spouses are quite commonplace. In instances like these, a diagnosis presumably pertaining to a patient's "disturbance" does not really describe a physical illness, but obscures the hidden violence and duplicity of family life and mandates treatments that compound the previous damage, rather than reverse it.

Psychiatrists take offense at this line of argument. They do not see themselves as being aligned with the old against the young, with men against women, the powerful against the powerless, and so on though many, by their own admission, lack the time, patience, sensitivity, and/or training to engage in the kind of careful inquiry that would really rule out such occurrences. "No, no," they say, "there just isn't time. And besides, why bother, when the disorder is invariably organic in nature?"

Is it? There is a lot at stake here, so let us proceed cautiously. Chapter 1 of *The Divided Self* invited readers to consider an ambiguous picture—one that could be construed alternately as a vase or chalice, or as two faces turned towards each other, but not as both simultaneously. Prior to its appearance in *The Divided Self,* this ambiguous figure was used by Gestalt psychologists to illustrate that perception is not merely the passive registration of external stimuli—mere "data collection"—as Lockean empiricism had suggested. On the contrary, perception is invariably an act of interpretation that integrates the data impinging on the senses in terms of a overall pattern or *Gestalt.* Which Gestalt you favor, at any given moment, determines what you see. This view of perception reverses the commonsense empiricist view that seeing is believing. In this case, the reverse is true: "I'll see it when I believe it."

Arguing by analogy with this figure, Laing declared that the schizophrenic patient can be seen either as a disordered organism or as a distressed, despairing person, but not as both simultaneously. The way in which we interpret the patient's behavior will determine *what* we see. In his own words, if one is listening to another person talking, one may be either (1) studying verbal behavior in terms of neural processes, or (2) trying to understand what he or she is saying. In the latter case, an explanation of verbal behavior in terms of the general nexus of organic changes that must necessarily be going on as a condition of his verbalization is no contribution to a possible understanding of what the individual is saying (Laing, 1960, p. 21).

Instead of pursuing explanation in causal/biological terms, Laing advocated the hermeneutic or *Verstehende* approach pioneered by German historian Wilhelm Dilthey. Dilthey argued that because the natural sciences employ experimental and quantitative research methods and aim to predict and control the behavior of the objects and processes in their domains, they are inappropriate to the study of human history, psychology, or art. The study of human minds and artifacts requires a separate and distinctive methodology, one that seeks to *understand* others rather than to predict and control their behavior. To understand others is to see their behavior and utterances humanly, as an expression of their experience of the world and of their intentions toward it, rather than as a sequence of mechanical or organismic processes governed by natural law (Makkreel, 1975).

Laing was not the first to introduce the *Verstehende* approach to psychiatry. In *General Psychopathology,* published in 1913, Karl Jaspers had stressed the usefulness of bracketing all naturalistic and causal preconceptions and attempting to understand the ideas, experiences, and intentions of patients in purely human terms. Perversely, however, Jaspers stipulated that empathy is of no avail in schizophrenia (Laing, 1964; 1982). According to Jaspers, clinicians can understand the subjective experience of severe disorders involving anxiety, depression, mania, and so on by analogy with their own affective states. But try as they might, they will never be able to bridge the "abyss" of understanding that separates the schizophrenic from the normal person.

Laing disagreed. Like Harry Stack Sullivan, he thought schizophrenics are "simply more human than otherwise" (Laing, 1963b). And unlike Jaspers, who sought to integrate Dilthey's *Verstehende* approach with causal and biological theories of mental disorder, Laing simply dropped the causal-biological standpoint altogether. Laing's radicalism on this point was brash and bracing. But leaving rhetoric aside, the *practical* relevance of Laing's critique became apparent in chapter 2 of *The Divided Self*. Laing's target there was Emile Kraepelin, who first differentiated between the catatonic, hebephrenic, and paranoid forms of *dementia praecox*.

Laing's vignette is a transcript of Kraepelin presenting a case of "catatonic excitement" to his students and colleagues. Kraepelin began by taking a disturbed youth—whom we'll call Hans—into a room full of specialists, interns, and students who were presumably total strangers. He then proceeded to describe Hans to this avid audience while trying to conduct a mental-status exam. The first thing Hans did when he entered the auditorium was to throw off his slippers, sing a hymn, and shout—in English, which was not his native tongue—"My father, my real father!" (Kraepelin did not note which hymn he sang). When asked where he is, noted Kraepelin, Hans shouted: "'I tell you who is being measured and is measured and shall be measured. I know all that, and could tell you, but do not want to.' When asked his name, he says: 'What is your name? What does he shut? He shuts his eyes. What does he hear? He does not understand . . . How? Who? Where? When? What does he mean? . . . I say, what is it then? Why do you give me no answer? . . . How can you be so impudent? I'm coming! I'll show you!'" (Laing, 1960, pp. 29–30).

Kraepelin found these remarks void of meaning. Laing, by contrast, said Hans was expressing his resentment at being studied in an impersonal, authoritarian manner. He did not want to be measured and tested. He wanted to be *heard* (Laing, 1960, p. 31).

Any hypotheses we conjure to account for Hans's behavior are bound to be highly conjectural. After all, Kraepelin did not provide us with any additional information, except to say that Hans was eighteen and apparently in splendid health. Laing, in turn, had no biographical information to add, and beyond noting the obvious did not venture to interpret what was going on between psychiatrist and patient. In retrospect, it is a pity that Laing did not press his advantage, since this exchange fairly cries out for more detailed analysis. Perhaps we can generate some plausible hypotheses to amplify Laing's perspective.

To begin with, Hans's dramatic entrance begs the question: Why the deliberate farce about mistaking Kraepelin for his father? In addition to love, fathers are supposed to give their sons protection, guidance, and discipline. By shouting "My father, my real father" (in English), maybe Hans was hinting that he hoped to discover these traits in Kraepelin but was afraid of saying so straightforwardly; he hoped instead that Kraepelin would sense his desire and his simultaneous need to disguise it. If this conjecture is correct, Hans's "inappropriate" exclamation was a shame-faced, adolescent way of telling us something, albeit elliptically, about the needs and hopes he was bringing to this strange situation.

Then again, given his age and circumstances, and the vehemence of his later remarks, it is more likely that Hans was mocking Kraepelin's paternalism—his *pretence* of fatherliness. If so, then Hans was saying—not in so many words, but as a meta-communication—that he is already disappointed in Kraepelin and holds him in contempt for his heartless "objectivity." Another, more intriguing possibility is that Hans's theatricality was less the expression of acutely felt needs and fears than an oblique commentary on the attitudes and feelings of the doctors and interns assembled by Kraepelin for this clinical demonstration. Perhaps Hans sensed a deep narcissistic hunger lurking behind Kraepelin's antiseptic clinicism and discerned that the real reason these strangers were staring so intently at him was not to help or understand, but to admire Kraepelin's clinical virtuosity. Perhaps Hans felt that the hushed veneration of Kraepelin's audience was childish and misplaced—transference?—and mocked them because their tendency to deify Kraepelin was slavish and tended to flatter Kraepelin's phantasies of omniscience.[3]

Finally, perhaps Hans hoped to convey (and/or conceal) *all* of these sentiments in his cryptic, heated declamations. This may well be so, since schizophrenic communication is seldom straightforward or univocal. On the contrary, it is elliptical and multivalent, and can be interpreted on several levels simultaneously. Nevertheless, even if Hans's affective state was inappropriate—a moot point, actually, depending on how you construe his situation—his communications, however unusual, are emphatically *not* senseless. On the contrary, they are fraught with meaning, even if anger, desperation, and fear hindered Hans's capacity to express himself more conventionally. Kraepelin's glib summation notwithstanding, it may be that Kraepelin was preconsciously aware of the latent implications of Hans's "ravings" and chose to punish the lad's impertinence by treating them as empty sound and fury and persuading others to do likewise.

To summarize then, Kraepelin described Hans's behavior in

Families, Phenomenology, and Schizophrenia · 69

terms of mental incapacity, while Laing construed it as an intelligible response to his situation. These divergent ways of seeing behavior and communication lead to radically different *practical* outcomes. Indeed, Laing observed: "It is just possible to have a thorough knowledge of what has been discovered about the hereditary or familial incidence of manic-depressive psychosis or schizophrenia, to have a facility in recognizing schizoid 'ego distortion' and schizophrenic ego defects, plus the various 'disorders' of thought, memory, perceptions, etc . . . without being able to understand a single schizophrenic. Such data are all ways of *not* understanding him" (Laing, 1960, p. 33).

So let us grant Laing's argument: mad or not, Hans's behavior is a function of his experience and intentions, and equally, one might add, of his neediness, defiance, and despair. And if one empathizes with the patient, then Hans's putative illness, his obvious inability to communicate effectively, is largely a function of *our* inability or unwillingness to understand *him*, rather than the other way around. The same is true, said Laing, for the vast majority of diagnostic and clinical situations involving alleged schizophrenics. But this fact is obscured by the assumptions that govern standard psychiatric practice, in which "the psychiatrist, as *ipso facto* sane, shows that the patient is out of contact with him. The fact that he is out of contact with the patient shows that there is something wrong with the patient, but not something wrong with the psychiatrist" (Laing, 1967, ch. 5).

In *The Oxford Companion to the Mind,* Laing summarized his view as follows:

> The attribution of the absence in the other of the capacity to form good enough personal relationships is the basis for the diagnosis of schizophrenia. This diagnosis is both an attribution (he is incapable of forming an interpersonal bond), and a causal theory to account for this attribution (the reason he is cut off is because he is suffering from a mental or physical illness).
>
> In *The Divided Self,* Laing construed this attribution as a function of an extremely disjunctive relationship between the person who is in the role of a depersonalized—and depersonalizing—diagnosing psychiatrist and the person who has become a depersonalized, and sometimes depersonalizing, diagnosed patient. This construction is a contribution towards a personal understanding (*Verstehen*) of what is

going on between psychiatrist and patient, in contrast to a scientific explanation of what is going on in the patient alone. In fact, he offered a personal understanding of the psychiatrist's scientific explanation and construed it as, unwittingly, a way of cutting off the cut-off person from the possibility of reunion and renewal. (Laing, 1987, p. 417)

In short, the clinical posture that Laing disparaged is one in which the clinician assumes a priori that he is a neutral scientific observer/classifier of an (irrational) patient's speech and behavior. The result, said Laing, is not a collaborative search for truth, but what Erving Goffman called "a degradation ceremonial." Indeed, at one point he was moved to say: "The countermadness of Kraepelinian psychiatry is the exact counterpart of 'official' psychosis . . . it is as *mad*, if by madness we mean radical estrangement from the totality of what is the case" (Laing, 1967, p. 142).

Utterances like these prompted the charge that Laing was romanticizing schizophrenia, a charge he steadfastly denied. But did he? If we are asking whether Laing minimized or denied the anguish and confusion that accompanies the various behaviors and states of mind we designate as schizophrenic, the answer is a simple and unqualified "no." Experientially, Laing never depicted schizophrenia as anything but a mixture of chronic fear, confusion, isolation, and despair, punctuated by relatively brief intervals of lucidity or ecstasy.

Laing recalled, however, that when he was training in psychiatry in 1950, many senior psychiatrists still said that if all schizophrenic patients were cared for respectfully in good-enough surroundings, one-quarter to one-third of them would eventually recover without the benefits of shock, drugs, or lobotomy—a view shared by *most* psychiatrists at the turn of the century (Laing, 1976).

Later, while training as an analyst, Laing came across many instances of spontaneous remission in which subjects were not merely restored to their premorbid condition, but emerged more integrated, insightful, and grounded than before—at least by their own reckoning. People like these experienced the symptoms of their disorder as the outward stigmata of a radical inner transformation, a tortured epiphany whose symbolic and existential significance registered only *after* their crisis began to abate. It had to be *lived* before it could be understood. Following Jung, Laing called this process "metanoia"—the ancient Greek word for "repentance."

Drawing on case histories, first-person accounts, and the reports of friends and patients who had metanoia-type experiences, Laing concluded that in optimal circumstances, a psychotic interlude can have potentially positive or redeeming characteristics, despite the suffering it entails. To wrestle a redemptive measure of freedom and insight from a psychotic interlude, and to halt the dreaded decline into chronicity, said Laing, the distressed and disoriented person needs both a perfectly safe, noncoercive environment and the supportive and nonintrusive presence of others who have also made this perilous inner journey and can act as guides, facilitators, and protectors.

Laing's enthusiasm for the metanoia concept was such that from 1964 to 1969 he supposed that most psychotic disturbances could be successfully resolved if only the requisite conditions were provided. During this phase, Laing was also apt to construe psychotics as reluctant explorers lost in the vastness of "inner space," and to disparage or dismiss any neurobiological account of the disorder. After 1969, however, Laing was more cautious. During the seventies, on several occasions, he publicly estimated the odds of spontaneous recovery at 50 percent or less, even under optimal conditions. And though he continued his opposition to electroshock, Laing was no longer opposed to the use of psychotropic medication, provided that patients were fully informed of potential side effects.

So if the question is whether Laing ever, at any time, romanticized schizophrenia, *despite the suffering it entails,* the answer, unfortunately, is "yes." From 1964 to 1969, Laing was "over the top," despite later disclaimers to the contrary. But though this explains the widespread tendency to dismiss Laing altogether, it does not excuse it. Much of Laing's critique of psychiatry during this period remains valid. Moreover, much of Laing's work was done *before* 1964, and though some of it prefigures *The Politics of Experience,* none of it romanticizes schizophrenia in any way. Indeed, the only reference to metanoia that appears in this body of work is chapter 5 of *Self and Others,* called "The Coldness of Death." There Laing did *not* suggest that the experience of Mrs. A was somehow representative. Instead, he merely depicted it as one possible outcome—a particularly instructive outcome—of a psychotic interlude.

Because of his scathing dismissals of biological psychiatry, it is important to remember that during the most productive and prolific decade of Laing's life, between 1960 and 1970, the physical evidence on behalf of the medical model was astonishingly flimsy. At that time, Laing was justified in treating the rigid insistence on the organic etiology of schizophrenia as a stubborn and irrational article of faith. Since the late 1970s, however, evidence has accumulated that buttresses the medical model in several ways (e.g., Mesulam, 1990). Still, as Louis Sass points out, important questions remain. While there are high correlations between certain kinds of brain defects and certain schizophrenic symptoms, not all people who have these defects are symptomatic. Conversely, not all of those who are symptomatic have these defects. Moreover, some of the defects in question are not specific to schizophrenia, but are found in other severe disorders as well. Finally, despite the recent breakthroughs, not one variety of schizophrenia listed in the *Diagnostic and Statistical Manual of Mental Disorders* has a proven etiology yet, so none of this work, however provocative, is definitive (Sass, 1992).

Another interesting development is the search for genetic predispositions to schizophrenia. For some unfathomable reason, until 1990 or so many researchers were confident that the alleged predisposition could be traced to a single gene, and most of them were betting on chromosome six. Then others chimed in insisting on a role for chromosome four. Nowadays, it is widely conceded that the search for a defect in a single gene is utterly pointless and that any genetic substrate to the disorder must involve at least four to six genes. Chromosomes four and six are still heavily implicated, but the others are hotly contested. And if *more* than six genes are involved—as may well be the case—it may take a while to sort out their role (Moldin and Gottesman, 1997).

Despite all the intrigue, ingenuity, and conceptual sophistication associated with this research, the fact remains that from a purely practical and/or therapeutic standpoint, the prospective yield from it is moot. The fact that someone has a predisposition to a specific disorder does not mean that he or she will necessarily acquire it, nor does it affect the clinical management of the case once symptoms have emerged. So what is the difference? Unless one is willing to sanction a massive exercise in genetic engineering—with God-knows-what unforeseen consequences—it is difficult to discern how this knowledge will help matters, or where it will lead (Skrabanek, 1997).

Admittedly, the fact that the genetics of schizophrenia may not have much practical relevance in treatment does not mean that the issue is sterile or baseless from a purely scientific point of view. There probably is a polygenetic predisposition to schizophrenia, and perhaps, sometime soon, it will be discovered. But what then? If a clear and uniform pattern emerges, the question will be: how much weight should we assign to this polygenetic predisposition relative to environmental factors? After all, over the last few decades, concordance rates for identical twins have hovered in the vicinity of 50 percent, indicating that environmental processes account for around half of the variance. With minor fluctuations, these findings have been remarkably stable over the last few decades. Yet if you follow the money, the vast preponderance of funds are devoted to biological research, while funds allocated for environmental factors have dwindled to almost nothing.

This is not a rational state of affairs. If empirical findings alone determined what is deemed worthy of research, one would expect a more equitable distribution of resources. Judging from the way money is allocated, however, our current research agenda is shaped more by political considerations than by genuinely scientific ones. To be blunt, one sometimes gets the impression that the vast amount of energy and resources devoted to this search is a collective effort to legitimate a particular view of schizophrenia—one that will save biological psychiatry's reputation and discredit competing views of the illness. In other words, biological psychiatrists seem to feel deeply threatened at the prospect of losing their hegemony and are out to clobber the competition (Skrabanek, 1997).

Still, it would be naive to dismiss the possibility that neurology and psychiatry may zero in on deficiencies or defects whose prevention or rectification could eliminate or dramatically reduce some problems currently classified as schizophrenic with fewer iatrogenic effects. This would be an improvement on the present state of affairs, where the side effects of medication—and thoughtless or punitive overmedicating, which is still shockingly routine all around the world—are horrifying (Cohen, 1990; Breggin, 1991). And this raises some complex and delicate questions about the current status of Laing's critique.

Unfortunately, most psychiatrists, psychologists, and researchers are inclined to think that there is nothing complicated or delicate about it. They simply think that recent developments vindicate the medical model and invalidate Laing's paranoid ravings once and for all. Another, smaller group has sufficient realism and generosity to concede that Laing's skepticism was once warranted by the state of the evidence, but suggest that in the current climate he is simply irrelevant—an intriguing footnote to psychiatric history, a casuality of scientific progress. Hugh Freeman, writing in the *Times Higher Education Supplement* (London), typified this attitude when he wrote: "Laing will continue to figure prominently in the cultural history of the later 20th century, and his early writings will continue to be of interest to those who seek to understand psychotic experience. But so far as the management of mental illness is concerned, he was a phenomenon that came and went" (May 16, 1997).

Others, including a handful of psychiatrists, think this triumphalism is a bit smug and premature. But sadly, Laing invited this kind of posthumous dismissal. Though he started out in a fairly cautious and circumspect manner, by the mid-sixties Laing had linked his views on schizophrenia and the micropolitics of the family and psychiatry with a sweeping denunciation of society at large (Burston, 1996a; Kotowicz, 1997). Though he later backed away from this posture somewhat, many readers recoiled from Laing's characterization of the twentieth century as "a veritable age of Darkness." And even when they welcomed this kind of global condemnation, as many did, many others were dismayed by the vehemence of Laing's characterization of the average marriage where, in his estimation:

> One is expected to be capable of passion, once married, but not to have experienced too much passion (let alone acted on it) too much before. If this is too difficult, one has to pretend first not to feel the passion one really feels, then to pretend to passion one does *not* really feel, and to pretend that passionate upsurges of resentment, hatred, envy, are unreal, or don't happen, or are something else. This requires false realizations, false de-realizations, and a cover story (rationalization). After this almost complete holocaust of one's experience on the altar of conformity, one is liable to feel somewhat empty, but one can try to fill one's emptiness up with money, consumer

goods, position, respect, admiration . . . These together with a reper-
toire of distractions, permitted or compulsory, serve to distract one
from one's own distraction. (Laing, 1971, pp. 100–101)

No doubt this scathing assessment was consonant with the temper
of the times, when the viability of monogamous marriage was
widely questioned. Still, even in the seventies, only a very angry and
very famous person could write like this and feel confident of getting a hearing. Though his honesty was commendable, perhaps,
public sentiment inevitably turned against, or at any rate, away
from him. Psychologically minded people, whether married or single, suspected autobiographical determinants, a personal axe to
grind, behind this devastating appraisal. People whose marriages
were rooted in genuine mutuality and affirmation dismissed it as
unduly pessimistic. Those unfortunate souls whose marriages fit
this grim pattern probably resented Laing's candor, unless of course
they were heading for a divorce. And finally, those whose marriages
wavered between inauthenticity and interludes of genuine meeting
rejected it on the grounds that it deprived them of hope for saving
or improving their marriages.

Perhaps on some level Laing sensed all of this. After all, in 1980,
with his fame now behind him, he assured Douglas Kirsner (in
Mullan, 1997) that he felt quite at home in contemporary civilization and believed—unlike Freud, for example—that a perfectly
"natural" and uncoerced love between a man and a woman can
still flourish and that many of the social changes wrought by the
twentieth century actually promote the emergence of such volun-
tary and loving unions. Indeed, Laing now insisted that his earlier
remarks on families and society generally had been widely mis-
interpreted. And in a synopsis of his life's work written for *The
Oxford Companion to the Mind,* published in 1987, Laing noted
plaintively that his thesis regarding the social intelligibility of
symptoms "is quite uncontentious and non-exclusive, but it has led
to a lot of controversy, and a lot of contentious misunderstanding"
(p. 418).

Clearly, Laing was unwilling or unable to acknowledge his own
role in igniting and fanning the ferocious controversies that sur-
rounded his work. And unfortunately, for various reasons, he was
unwilling or unable to continue his family research after 1964.
Moreover, the lively antipathies he engendered, and the uniqueness

of his approach, have effectively precluded others from following in his footsteps. Recent research on the impact of "expressed emotion" in the families of schizophrenics, and on the way that open expression of negative or critical feelings by family members fosters regression and recidivism (for example, Leff and Vaughn, 1985) are scarcely worth mentioning in this context. There is nothing wrong with this research; it is perfectly valid, as far as it goes. But it asks different questions, employs different methods, and brings different phenomena to light. As a result, it cannot be invoked to support or refute any of Laing's central theses regarding mystification, invalidation, double binds, false and untenable positions, intergenerational transmission, and so on. Strictly speaking, it is completely and utterly beside the point, and those who invoke these disparate bodies of research in the same breath—to vindicate or dismiss Laing—must contrive some rather forced and superficial comparisons in order to say anything at all. (Why bother?)

A more natural and instructive comparison would be between Laing's ideas and Bowlby's work on families (see, for example, Bowlby, 1988, chs. 5 and 6). Though he never acknowledged it in print, Bowlby told me personally that Laing exerted a very strong influence on him, and that he regarded *Sanity, Madness, and the Family* as the most important book on families written this century. Still, the fact remains that such influence is devilishly difficult to detect because Bowlby focused on the remediation of families where the violence and neglect are *overt*, and where the traumas inflicted by parents on their children (and one another) are potentially recoverable as memories of discrete historical events. In other words, Bowlby's patients were generally violated physically in ways they may or may not remember, but that other family members routinely deny. Such scenarios are scarce among Laing's clinical profiles. As a rule, Laing's patients were violated emotionally by perverse patterns of relatedness that they cannot distinctly remember: indeed they can scarcely imagine them, because our culture *still* lacks the vocabulary to describe the many forms of mental anguish they underwent. In addition to addressing a kind of cultural alexithymia, Laing's clinical formulations lay bare the subtle but profound consequences of *self-inflicted* violence—that is, the patient's denial and invalidation of his or her *own* experience on the altar of conformity.

None of this detracts from Bowlby's contribution, of course. His work on family violence was deep and discerning, and one would be childish to dispute its merit. But Laing elucidated subtler, more elusive forms of violence that are generally neither apparent to external observers, nor detectable and measurable in the standard empirical research formats in which Bowlby excelled. But the reverse is also true: if Laing probed areas of human experience and interaction that were inaccessible to Bowlby, he did not give *overt* violence and neglect their due. Theoretically, the ideal would be an integrated approach. From a purely historical point of view, it is intriguing to note that these two pioneers worked in such close proximity for so long without palpably affecting one another's research methodologies. And this, in turn, calls attention to another striking feature of Laing's legacy: that all of the criticism he garnered concerned his (real or alleged) conclusions, rather than his *methodology*, which was never seriously addressed, not even by Bowlby (see, for example, Frank, 1990).

Whatever their shortcomings, Bowlby's views on research methodology were remarkably clear. As Laing pointed out, Bowlby regarded biology and ethology as the parent disciplines for mental health research, and regarded the "historical" or social sciences as being secondary and as having nothing distinctive to contribute outside the realm of psychotherapy, where personal and family "history" shape the vagaries of individual symptoms (for example, Bowlby, 1988, ch. 4). With Laing, the emphasis is reversed. The parent discipline is philosophy, and the way in which a family functions is not the expression of (or deviation from) some overarching biological imperative, but the result of a complex interweaving of intergenerational effects blending with and modified by the effects of concerted individual agency.

Unlike his views on individual therapy, which were rooted in existentialism and to a lesser extent in psychoanalysis, Laing's family theory was rooted primarily in phenomenology, and secondarily in psychoanalysis. As indicated earlier, phenomenology is an approach that stresses the existence of a world of immediate or "lived" experience that precedes the objectified and abstract world of natural-scientific inquiry. Its purpose is to illumine and describe the most intimate interstices of this experiential realm, rather than to explain it in causal or scientific terms. This recourse to detailed description is not an irrationalist exercise, a sweeping subjectivism, or an undignified surrender to the arbitrary whims and parochial perspectives of particular observers. On the contrary, claim phenomenologists, rigorous phenomenological observation and description can clear away all that rubbish and yield surprisingly robust results.

Laing was the not the first to study schizophrenia phenomenologically. But he was the first to study the families of people diagnosed this way. With the partial exception of Eugene Minkowski, whose work Laing admired (Laing, 1963a), Laing's approach to phenomenology was quite different from his predecessors'. For one thing, as he noted in *The Divided Self,* he was cheerfully eclectic. He was simply not interested in a pure or rigorous application of any single philosopher's views to the study of mental disorder. Another difference lay in his attitude toward the concept of psychopathology. After all, any theory of psychopathology (and its accompanying taxonomy of disorders) entails a host of normative and theoretical preconceptions that act as a kind of template or filter, which distorts the clarity and immediacy of experience that phenomenology is intended to achieve. So what is the alternative? In essence, when dealing with deeply disturbed individuals, Laing attempted to implement Husserl's *epoche*—the bracketing of any beliefs and preconceptions embedded in the "natural" or "scientific" attitudes. Rather than viewing the bizarre utterances and ideas of patients as merely "crazy" or as the expression of a brain disorder, the clinician should seek to understand a patient's behavior in light of his experience and intentions toward the world, without imputing the existence of unconscious "mechanisms" (such as projection, denial, and regression) to account for his experience or behavior.

But Husserlian (or transcendental) phenomenology is essentially monadological: it is only designed to elucidate the operations of one consciousness at a time. This was not problematic at first, since most of the clinical material Laing used in *The Divided Self* was derived from individual psychotherapy cases. Admittedly, even here, the connection between disturbed and disturbing ideas and behavior and early childhood experiences was patent. But at this point, the phenomenological component of his thought was still quite secondary to the existential element, and Laing could afford to treat parental imagos as the intentional correlates of the patient's own mental activities, and to bracket questions of veracity and/or historical actuality.

In the eleventh and final chapter of *The Divided Self,* however—the case of Julie—Laing was already chafing against the constraints of this individualistic approach. Accordingly, without noting his shift in perspective, he leapt outside this individual framework to study the relationships between the patient, her mother, and her sister as they were occurring. To elucidate the context in which Julie's symptoms became intelligible—that is, why she claimed her mother was trying to kill her, or indeed, already had—Laing could no longer treat significant others as imagos or intentional correlates. Nor was it sufficient to take an "individual" history. Laing had to study the family's experience of Julie, as well as her experience of them. Or, to put it more precisely, Laing had to clarify the nature and timing of the transformations in their experience of her—transformations that had prompted her mother's successive characterizations of her daughter as "good," "bad," and "mad," and had issued ultimately in Julie's hospitalization. He also had to track the corresponding transformations in Julie's experience of her mother and other family members while these events took place. As a result, this chapter reads like a preliminary sketch for *Sanity, Madness and the Family*—and a brilliant sketch it is.

By this point, Laing doubtlessly realized that to achieve his purposes, he required a method that is transpersonal or interexperiential and had to search beyond Husserl for a firm theoretical foundation. Laing took two steps in this direction in *Self and Others* (1961). There he borrowed an algebraic notation developed by Martin Buber to visually depict the interplay of experience, fantasy, and communication between *two* people. This was progress, but of a limited kind, since families seldom consist of a single, discrete dyad. So toward the end of this same book, in chapter 9, Laing took Bateson's "double bind" hypothesis on board. (As with Buber's interpersonal algebra, Laing modified and expanded appreciably on Bateson's original formulation in the years that followed.)

Methodologically, Laing's debts to Buber and Bateson are certainly worthy of further discussion. But his greatest single debt was to Sartre, whose book *Critique of Dialectical Reason* he and David Cooper summarized in *Reason and Violence: A Decade of Sartre's Philosophy* (1964). For reasons that are not terribly relevant here, Sartre was dissatisfied with the extant Marxist theories of ideology, "class consciousness," solidarity, mass action, and so on. He did not wish to jettison them entirely, but because of existentialism's characteristic individualism, its distrust of collectivism, and his own anti-essentialist stance, Sartre developed a concept of human groups as closely interdigitated *series* of individuals. He used the word "series" deliberately to avoid treating a group as a unified or singular entity, thereby losing sight of the individuals who compose it.

Sartre's modifications to historical materialism hinged on the idea that group process, as it is called, is really an alienated apperception of concerted individual *practices*. So what appears to happen in a group anonymously, without anyone understanding or intending what is happening, can ultimately be traced back to the individual projects and experienced needs of those who compose it, within the framework of constraints provided by (generally scarce) material resources and the simultaneous efforts and desires of all the others who comprise a group (Laing and Cooper, 1964; Soper, 1986).

Though quite schematic and deficient for the purposes Sartre had intended (Soper, 1986), this nominalistic theory of groups as complex, contradictory multiplicities appealed to Laing because it avoided positing the existence of (1) a collective subject, collective unconscious, or "group mind," or (2) a set of group "dynamics" separate from and superordinate to the individuals who compose it, or (3) regulatory structures or systems—analogous to organic ones—that channel energy and information and operate on the basis of inertia, homeostatis, and so forth. In addition, by resolving "process" back into the concatentation of individual practices (including beliefs, experiences, decisions, and utterances), and by situating the individual within this collectively constructed framework, it promised to illumine the patient's "situation," which is as opaque to him or her as it is to the other family members.

Leaving Buber and Bateson aside, then, the key constitutive elements of Laing's "social phenomenology" are derived from Husserl and Sartre. From Husserl, Laing adopted the habit of bracketing theoretical presuppositions, rather than allowing them to inflect (or infect) what he actually observed. From Sartre he adapted a method for analyzing seemingly anonymous and/or unconscious group processes, a method that avoided endowing the group itself with subjectivity, or indeed, with a pseudo-objectivity (an essential nature or structure that is separate or superordinate to the people who actually compose it). These influences are vividly apparent throughout *Sanity, Madness and the Family*, but especially in the introduction, where Laing wrote:

> The judgement that the diagnosed patient is behaving in a biologically dysfunctional (hence pathological) way is, we believe, premature, and one we hold in parentheses.
>
> Although we ourselves do not accept the validity of the clinical terminology, it is necessary to establish . . . that the persons whose families we are describing are as "schizophrenic" as anyone is. By "schizophrenic" we mean here a person who has been diagnosed as such and has come to be treated accordingly . . . We reiterate that we are not using the term "schizophrenia" to denote any identifiable condition that we believe exists "in" one person. However, in so far as the term summarizes a set of clinical attributions made by certain persons about the experience and behavior of others, we retain the term for this set of attributions . . .
>
> After recording these attributions, we have then described the family relationships phenomenologically. Neither *organic* pathology, nor *psycho* pathology, nor for that matter *group* pathology is assumed to be or not to be in evidence. The issue is simply bracketed off. (Laing and Esterson, 1964, pp. 18–19)

In addition to "bracketing," Laing and Esterson credited Sartre with providing ideas and inspiration, and reflected on family processes in the following way:

> If one wishes to know how a football team concert or disconcert their actions in play, one does not think only or even primarily of approaching this problem by talking to the members individually. One watches the way they play together.
>
> Most of the investigations of families of "schizophrenics," while contributing original and useful data to different facets of the problem, have not been based on direct observation of the members of the family together as they actually interact with each other.
>
> The way in which a family deploys itself in space and time, what space, what time, and what things are private or shared, and by whom—these and many other questions are best answered by seeing what sort of world the family has itself fleshed out for itself, both as a whole and differentially for each of its members.
>
> One does not wish, however, to study the system-properties of a

family abstracted from the experience and actions of the individuals whose continued living together in a particular way alone guarantees the continuance of this system . . .

Phenomenologically, a group can feel to its members like an organism; to those outside it, it can appear to act like one. But to go beyond this, and maintain that, *ontologically*, it is an organism, is to become completely mystified . . .

The concept of family *pathology* is, therefore, we believe, a confused one. It extends the unintelligibility of individual behavior to the unintelligibility of the group. It is the *biological analogy* applied now not just to one person, but to a multiplicity of persons . . . Not the individual but the family, therefore, needs the clinician's services to "cure" it: the family (or even society at large) is now a sort of hyperorganism with a physiology and pathology that can be well or ill. One arrives at a pan-clinicism, so to say, that is more a system of values than an instrument of knowledge. (Laing and Esterson, 1964, pp. 22–23).

In other words, according to Laing, clinicians who speak of diverse kinds of "family pathology" are not really analyzing family structures. Instead, they are *analogizing* and mistaking their metaphors for existential actualities. These metaphors may be illuminating and instructive, up to a point, but if taken at face value they are also misleading and apt to conceal all kinds of prescriptive value judgments under the guise of disinterested clinical observation and description.

These reflections enable us, finally, to flesh out the areas of convergence and divergence between Laing and other family theorists. Like Goffman, Bateson, and most family theorists, Laing insisted that with deeply disturbed patients, including schizophrenics, the primary locus of the disturbance does not usually reside in the brain or body of the individual, or even in the individual unconscious. On the contrary, the irrationality of the identified patient becomes vividly intelligible in light of the various pressures, constraints, and anomalies of communication to which he or she is subject to in his or her family of origin.

In order to ferret out these pressures, constraints, and anomalies, Laing agreed, it is necessary to study the family itself in action, and not just to interview individual members. Indeed, Laing went a step beyond his contemporaries by visiting families in their own homes, whenever possible. But in interpreting the data of this research, Laing eschewed organicist metaphors for group processes. Strictly speaking, there is no such thing as "family pathology," because the family is not an organism. Nor indeed, is it a thing, but a system of relations collaboratively created and sustained by all members concurrently, even in situations of acute conflict or mutual misunderstanding.

As a result, readers of *Sanity, Madness, and the Family* will find incisive descriptions of individual behavior that strike them as irrational, immoral, or perverse. But they will search Laing's work in vain for any taxonomy of family ills, for any (overt or hidden) prescriptions as to how a "healthy" family functions. In the absence of any prescriptive "models" of family functioning to illustrate his ideas, Laing's readers had to content themselves with a laborious methodology that was not without problems. To his credit, Laing was candid about these shortcomings. As we see below, some are raised in the introduction to *Sanity, Madness and the Family,* and others are hinted at in *The Oxford Companion to the Mind,* where he noted that

> The field of social phenomenology has been cultivated from the standpoints of anthropology, sociology, psychology, and philosophy. Any work in social phenomenology from any one of these points of view has implications for all the perspectives which are knit together by the common discipline of social phenomenology . . . The philosophy, anthropology, sociology, and psychology of interpersonal relations are all in an unsatisfactory state despite the . . . insights and intuitions of Hegel, Dilthey, Buber, Goffman, Husserl, Freud, Schutz, Marx, Nietzsche, Scheler, Heidegger, Sartre, Foucault, Merleau-Ponty, Bateson, MacMurray, and others, in and out of phenomenology, who have influenced Laing's work . . . the problems of method are as vexing as they are unresolved. In some instances they have not yet even been explicitly formulated. (Laing, in Gregory, 1987, p. 417)

The fact that methodological problems and controversies still bedevil the phenomenological field, as Laing acknowledged, is neither surprising nor cause for reproach. There are few fields, even in the natural sciences, where complete clarity and a calm, unbroken consensus regarding methodology prevails for long. On the contrary, progress depends on competing models. Unfortunately, detailed discussion of most of these issues is beyond our purview here. I merely address some of the more obvious ones that do not require a deep or extensive knowledge of phenomenology to grasp.

In the introduction to *Sanity, Madness and the Family,* Laing and Esterson cautioned that their findings are presented with a minimum of interpretation, whether existential or psychoanalytic. The reason, they said, is that analysts typically make inferences and attributions about the motives, meanings, and defenses informing behavior that the subjects of such analysis generally disavow. By adhering solely to ideas, motives, and experiences that family members freely concede, they said, they avoided potentially intractable issues of validation "that do not arise at the purely phenomenological level." Nevertheless, they noted that no researcher could deal adequately with an issue like sexuality in these families "unless they were willing to attribute to the agents involved fantasies of which they themselves are unconscious." As a result, they added, "the reader will find documented the quite manifest contradictions that beset these families, without very much exploration of the underlying factors which may be supposed to generate and maintain them" (p. 26).

These statements are striking for several reasons. First, Laing and Esterson eschewed inferences and attributions about unconscious motives, meanings, and defenses because they are supposedly off-limits to rigorous phenomenological inquiry. By their reckoning, once you invoke the unconscious, you are not practicing phenomenology; you are engaged in conjecture. No matter how plausible your conjecture may be, in view of circumstances, if a hypothetical mental process (or content) does not register in a person's conscious awareness, it is inadmissible and irrelevant to the matters at hand. (I tend to agree with this position, but in fairness to others, it entails a definition of phenomenological method that many today regard as too narrow—such as Walsh, 1996).

Second, Laing and Esterson freely concede that phenomenological method, though admirably suited to their immediate purpose, has palpable limitations as well. Indeed, with that thought in mind, they added that they hope to return to these cases some day, to offer more substantial psychodynamic interpretations. Yet curiously, that very same year, in the introduction to *Reason and Violence: A Decade of Sartre's Philosophy,* Laing and Cooper remarked that "there is plenty of room for a phenomenological investigation of 'unconscious phantasy,' in so far as the latter is conceived in its reality as experience and not as a series of mechanisms to be imposed on a subject objectified in the psycho-analytic situation. One might, on this point, propose a marriage between existential analysis and the structuralism of Jacques Lacan, who so expertly articulates the 'language' of the unconscious. Petty disputation regarding 'history' or 'History' should not delay the ceremony" (Laing and Cooper, 1964, p. 25).

This is another remarkable statement, because it reveals a profound disparity in the characterization of the nature and scope of phenomenology in these nearly simultaneous publications. In *Sanity, Madness and the Family,* "the unconscious" is just not kosher. In *Reason and Violence,* it is—or could be, at any rate, subject to certain conditions. At issue here is a tension between a predominantly Husserlian and/or Sartrean version of phenomenology, where unconscious processes are deemed worthless (or worse), and one akin to the work of Maurice Merleau-Ponty, who embraced Freud, in many ways, and who goes curiously unacknowledged here.

Why was Merleau-Ponty slighted? In all probability, his probing reflections on Freud were not accorded the attention they deserved because of the personal and political tensions that estranged Sartre from Merleau-Ponty in the mid-1950s. Praising Merleau-Ponty in a book devoted to celebrating Sartre's genius would have offended Sartre, and Laing probably preferred tact to perfect honesty on this occasion. Perhaps Lacan was less offensive to Sartre. Or perhaps, for reasons he did not articulate explicitly, Laing briefly felt that a synthesis of existential analysis with Lacanian thought really *would* expedite the integration of the theory of unconscious phantasy into phenomenology.

In retrospect, of course, it transpires that Laing's impetuous proposal of marrying the two approaches was not preceded by a patient and thoughtful courtship, as decorum demands, but was accompanied by an implied reproach for pettiness that Lacan would not have appreciated. Perhaps Lacan sensed some ambivalence here. And perhaps Laing *intended* his offer to fail, on some level. In any case, nothing came of it, and eventually Laing became as disenchanted with Lacan as he did with Cooper, though for different reasons.

Still, before we consign this curious proposal to the dustbin of history, it is useful to ponder Laing's motives for this surprising utterance. No doubt the initial attraction Laing and Cooper felt toward Lacanian theory was prompted by Lacan's antinomian concept of the ego and his scathing denunciation of the project of "normalization" that most analysts, psychiatrists, and psychologists embrace unreflectively in their clinical work. This attitude was admirably summed up by Stuart Schneiderman in *Jacques Lacan: The Death of an Intellectual Hero.*

> The scientific truths of psychology concern classes and categories of people within specific situations that are measurable. If human experience is not measurable, if a part of it does not show up in the data, the psychologist may arrogantly assume that it does not exist. Analysts know well that the best interpretations are not those that echo some bit of knowledge gleaned from a textbook. Instead they speak to the analysand as a singular subject. When psychology defines normal stages of human development and when therapists attempt to make sense of their patients' experience by referring them to some putative normality, then what they are doing is finding a convenient place for their patients within the concept they have of humanity. They teach their patients to identify with mankind. This is [an] identification that patients in analysis do not seek and should not be encouraged to develop. Such an identification is nothing more or less than the repression of subjectivity, of personal style, of quirks and idiosyncrasies.
>
> People who present themselves for psychoanalysis are said to be alienated from the norm. Perhaps this is true, but that does not justify attempting to reinsert them in that norm. (Schneiderman, 1984, pp. 111–112)

As we will see in Chapter 5, these sentiments resonate deeply with Laing's perspective, and for good reason. But the emphasis on the non-quantifiable, irreducibly subjective, and singular nature of personal experience, of not assimilating to the "crowd," and so on, are not uniquely Lacanian. On the contrary, they are old existentialist tropes that date back to Kierkegaard. Having said that, however, there are two problems with Schneiderman's position. First, as Schneiderman himself will concede by now, Lacanian theory lends itself to precisely the kinds of abuses that Lacan and his followers deplored by generating a plethora of airy generalizations that are elusive, abstruse, and remote from experience.

Second, as Suzanne Kirschner has shown recently (1996), the attempt to interpret personal experience within the framework of ostensibly normal developmental stages can be liberating as well as repressive. The concepts of humanity (or developmental schemata) that therapists cherish are seldom so disjunctive with the cultural preconceptions of their patients that they need to be imposed in this arbitrary fashion. Nor are patients so singular by nature that they lack the desire, the ability, or the need to understand and interpret their experience in terms of prevailing cultural categories. In most instances, as Kirschner observes, the developmental schemata that analysts bring to clinical work are culturally congruent, though their rootedness in prevailing folk psychology is not apparent to practitioners or patients, as a rule. Moreover, notes Kirschner, these developmental constructs not only sanction prevailing norms. In truth, their appeal often resides in the fact that they make allowance for generic human needs and tendencies that are misjudged and mishandled in the cultural mainstream and contain a tacit critique of the ways in which prevailing cultural norms lack realism and generosity.

Admittedly, none of this excuses the concerted adoption of an unreflective program of normalization or "adjustment," which with minor exceptions *was* the program of the mental health industry—and still is, for the most part. As we see in Chapter 5, concepts of normality are exceedingly diverse and ambiguous, and lend themselves to all kinds of repressive uses. But by the same token, respect for the individual should not prompt us to make a fetish of subjectivity and imagine that one tries to make sense of oneself, one's experience, and more specifically, one's suffering, in terms of concepts and norms that are completely at variance with those of the culture at large.

But before we got sidetracked on the issue of normalization, and of Laing's odd overture to Lacan, we were concerned with a methodological issue: the tension between a vision of a "pure" phenomenology that excludes the unconscious, and a more accommodating and flexible version that includes it, albeit with reservations and subject to certain conditions. Lest we forget, Sartre's *Being and Nothingness* proscribes the invocation of the unconscious to account for behavior that results from self-deception or "bad faith." Though he did not call attention to this fact, Laing was not really Sartrean in this respect. Far from it. Even in instances where he banned recourse to unconscious mental processes on methodological grounds, implying that phenomenology has no place for the unconscious, he granted their existence and their central role in human affairs.

Another problem in Laing's family theory that involves psychoanalysis emerged later that decade, in *The Politics of the Family*. In chapter 1, entitled "The Family and the 'Family,'" Laing differentiated between the actual, empirical family and the collective image or phantasy of the family internalized by its members, called the "family." The "family" is subject to idealization and distortion of various kinds and is roughly equivalent to what other family theorists term "the family myth." Laing felt that getting the family "out of your system" is an integral part of psychotherapy, the achievement of insight and relief from inner torment. If that process precipitates the loss of illusions, or creates greater emotional or geographical distance between the patient and his family, so be it. (But again, unlike David Cooper, Laing was *not* calling for the abolition of the family per se.)

Having made this point, Laing then emphasized that the "family" is not only internalized by introjection and identification, as psychoanalysis insists. In analytic lore, the terms introjection and identification describe the psychic assimilation of individual traits that are experienced, idealized, envied, and/or feared in the other—usually a parent. Laing stipulated that the "family" does not merely consist of representations of parents, but of parents, siblings, and possibly extended family members in stereotypical patterns of relationship—patterns that are initially suffered passively, but are later enacted in the symptoms of the patient. Here is a relatively transparent example.

A young man feels his life has come to a stop. He is preoccupied by the conflict between East and West, the cold war, the balance of terror, techniques of deterrence, one world, the impossibility of divorce, the need for co-existence, the apparent impossibility of co-existence. He has a mission to find a solution, but he feels hopeless, and paralysed. He does nothing, but feels crushed by his responsibility for the destruction he feels is inevitable.

The structural elements of his preoccupations—conflict, the cold war, emotional divorce, balance of terror, need for co-existence— resemble those in the relationship between his parents.

But he does not see those resemblances. He insists that his preoccupation with the world situation is not only entirely justified by the objective facts but entirely based on them. The world situation is a fact and thousands of people come from families like his, *therefore* there is no connection. (Laing, 1970, pp. 8–9)

There is nothing in this clinical vignette to surprise a psychoanalyst. Judging from the description, this patient, though troubled, is idealistic, well read, articulate—in short, "high functioning." The source of his anguish is obvious. His concerns about the arms race represent the projection of intrapsychic contents derived from the "cold war" between his parents. Despite a pervasive depressive theme and intermittent episodes of panic, helplessness, and hopelessness, there is no evidence of regression or paranoia, and the congruence between his unconscious representations and the pattern of world events is so close that he must be quite intelligent. His "ego" is relatively intact, and possibly much better than average in certain respects. The question then emerges—which world power represents the mother, and which the father? Which does he fear most? And in the event of a serious conflict, to whom does he give his primary allegiance—mother Russia, or Uncle Sam? (Probably the old Oedipus at the root of it all.)

But suppose this patient—call him Edward—who has impressed us so far with his moral earnestness and diligent command of facts, suddenly claims that he, and he alone, has the formula for world peace and that unbeknownst to their governments, rogue elements from the CIA and KGB, who know who he is, have developed a plot to discredit, persecute, and kill him, if need be. These delusions—of grandeur, persecution, reference, and so on—are attributed to a failure of reality testing occasioned by regression to a pre-Oedipal level. The presumption now is that Edward's phantasies and projections are more pathological, more distorted, and more "primitive" due to impaired ego functioning. Right?

Wrong, said Laing. Laing always regarded unconscious phantasy as a palimpsest for interpersonal experience, and with rare exceptions eschewed both ontogenetic and phylogenetic explanations for them.[4] Even with psychotic individuals, Laing was able to link the vagaries and vicissitudes of phantasy to the texture of lived experience—experience lost to consciousness not because of repression or denial, but because of the conjoint effects of mystification, invalidation, injunctions and attributions, and rules and meta-rules reverberating through the whole family system (Laing, 1971). The patient's parents were the principle figures in these dramas, though aunts, uncles, and siblings were also frequently involved. So in Edward's case, for example, the CIA and KGB might represent his parents' parents, siblings, or others with power and influence within the extended family who prefer that the marital couple remain estranged but who keep their intentions concealed, even from themselves, in order to succeed.

The main point is that in Laing's able hands, patients' phantasies acquired an uncanny degree of intelligibility in light of their parents' phantasies about them, and indeed, about the parents' own parents—the patient's grandparents (or the like). So if, on inquiry, a parent insisted that his or her disturbed child "takes after" their own mother or father, grandmother or father, or another relative, it often transpired that the patient had been scripted—or perhaps, unwittingly conscripted—into the performance of roles in an *intergenerational* drama of unknown age and provenance. To keep a drama this complex going, its participants have to internalize more than mere imagos of significant others: they have to internalize the rules regulating the commerce and conflicts between them all, and induce others to embody the characteristic attitudes and behavior patterns of people they have frequently never even met.

So far, some say, Laing was merely adding a new twist to the standard psychoanalytic approach (Frank, 1990). But Laing clearly thought otherwise and was quick to point out that the processes of "mapping" and induction he described do *not* entail the introjection or spontaneous identification of the young with elders who are loved or feared, but the deliberate (if unconscious) insertion of the individual into a complex network of communicating nodes of phantasy—a *social* phantasy system, not an intrapsychic one. As a result, by his reckoning, even normal people live in a quasi-hypnoid state for most of their lives and mistake their trancelike existences for authentic selfhood until nightmarish things begin to happen.

Moreover, unlike Freud, Laing was not anxious to derive all "family romances" from a single, Oedipal formula; he insisted instead that every case is unique and that the purpose of research is not to confirm a theoretical preconception but to discover what is actually the case. The most puzzling thing about Laing's work, however, is the almost complete lack of attention it has received.

Though not congenial to everyone, Laing's intergenerational perspective was far less ambiguous than Lacanian theory. Yet publications for and against Lacan continue to flow in bewildering profusion, while Laing's best work in this area languishes in obscurity, waiting for the world to rediscover it and to grapple with it constructively. One wonders who will rise to the challenge. Family therapists cannot be bothered because empirical phenomenological research is so labor intensive. And though they never say so, Laing's critique of organicist metaphors, and of their habitual alliances with parents, poses a threat to "business as usual" if taken too seriously. Lacanians, who have more invested in theory per se, would also be challenged by a rigorous application of Laingian phenomenology.

Leaving guild wars and rivalries aside, for the moment, there are also some good and relatively transparent reasons why Laing's work on intergenerational effects has not received more attention. One is that his whole approach is at variance with a commonsense notion of intergenerational identification that contains an important grain of truth. Despite Laing's trenchant observations on the intergenerational transmission of personality traits, of patterns of conflict and relatedness, and so on, the fact remains that children do identify with their parents (or grandparents) spontaneously, without always having their roles and ideals thrust on them by others (Ricoeur, 1970). This was not even Freud's discovery. It was a fact noted by J. H. Pestalozzi, Gabriel Tarde and Gustav Le Bon, G. Stanley Hall, J. M. Baldwin, and G. H. Mead (among others) under the heading of "imitation." Imitation is observable on the level of manifest behavior, but its effects in childhood go much deeper than that. In adopting and rehearsing the various roles and attitudes of adult models, children take an *active* role in their own socialization (Mead, 1934). We may blame parents for setting a bad example, but the fact remains that imitation is something that children do spontaneously. It is not something done *to* them.[5]

At the risk of overstating my case, there is one more factor to be taken into consideration. Quite apart from the vagaries of role playing, overt imitation, and so on, identification with one's elders is quite *likely* to occur if a child has an affinity with an elder based on genetically inherited traits that color his or her aptitudes and disposition, and/or a marked physical resemblance to the family member (Rycroft, 1973). Oddly Laing took no notice of this. Take the case of David Clark in Laing's "Intervention in Social Situations" (1971), a somewhat neglected but important paper. David was a nine-year-old boy with a tentative diagnosis of incipient schizophrenia who had been referred to Laing for a second opinion. His symptoms included a strong disinclination to attend school, where he was described as "irritable, distractible and restless," and a stubborn defiance of his mother's wishes and commands. He was out "at all hours" and did not come home regularly, even for meals. To add insult to injury, David simply did not care if his mother was angry or upset about his behavior, and he refused to talk to the first psychiatrist who saw him. On the positive side, everyone who knew him conceded that he was mechanically and artistically inclined, generally quite cheerful, and not involved in any criminal or antisocial behavior as far as anyone knew.

Nowadays, of course, David Clark would probably be given a double diagnosis of attention deficit disorder and conduct disorder, and promptly put on Ritalin. Those diagnoses were not fashionable then, however, and Laing worried that in the hands of the proper authorities, the diagnosis of incipient schizophrenia would inevitably become a self-fulfilling prophecy. Accordingly, Laing visited the Clarks' home and interviewed the boy's mother, father, two elder brothers, and younger sister for two and a half hours. He also had a brief "man to man" chat with David and learned that this truant youngster was often at a nearby building site, helping the local laborers with their tasks.

Toward the end of these discussions, Laing asked Mrs. Clark: "Who do your children take after?" The eldest son, by common consent, took after his father, while the second took after nobody, apparently. David, it transpired, actually took after his mother— not as she was presently, but as a younger child, before she was beaten into being "good" by her own mother. And who, asked Laing, did Mrs. Clark take after? Her own father, she replied, who died just before David was conceived. On further inquiry, Mrs. Clark described her father as an easygoing man who had earned just enough money to meet his financial and familial obligations, and was answerable to no one—especially his wife—about his whereabouts or activities during his frequent absences from home. He never learned to read or write, but Mrs. Clark had loved and emulated him just the same, until her mother beat her black and blue. Evidently, Mrs. Clark lacked the resolve to beat the "bad-ness" out of David as her mother had beat it out of her, which is why she had called on the authorities to intervene.

Laing came to believe that Mrs. Clark had unconsciously *in-duced* her son David to replace her beloved father, who had died just prior to David's conception. And perhaps indeed she had. Per-haps on some level, Mrs. Clark desperately needed her father's continuing presence in her life, even after she had consciously em-braced her mother's negative appraisal of him. But Laing made no effort to explain how Mrs. Clark had induced David to "take af-ter" his grandfather, leaving us to infer that she had embarked on a process analogous to hypnotic induction, albeit unconsciously, over many years.

In any event, said Laing, it would be wrong to speak of identi-fication here—a point well taken, since identification is an intra-psychic process, not an interpersonal one, and since David never knew his grandfather, nor had any experience of his mother while she was (consciously) taking after him. Laing's logic was sound, then, at least in this case. Nevertheless, it is instructive to note that Laing simply ignored the possibility that David and his grandfather shared genetically based temperamental traits that his mother may have detected when he was young, and that this dimly apperceived fact could have been the "reality hook" on which she hung her elaborate projections.

Admittedly, as Laing observed, parents often secretly coerce their children into acquiring and enacting the traits and attitudes of their own parents and siblings by using attributions and injunc-tions, placing them in false and untenable positions, and subjecting them to unspoken rules (and metarules) governing what can or cannot be thought, felt, or expressed in the family circle (Laing, 1961; 1971). These processes of stereotyping and psychic impris-onment are vividly apparent in disturbed families and (in less vivid form) in normal families too. But this is not the whole story, espe-cially in societies like ours, where families are obliged by economic pressures to adapt to rapidly changing social and technological re-alities. The family is not a closed system and cannot possibly repli-cate its role-repertoires blindly and perfectly without handicapping its members. Even in stable societies, where the pace of social change is slow and modulated by tradition, children write their own life scripts, to a certain extent—despite the fact that they have acquired many genetically inherited aptitudes or traits acquired from their forebears.

So Laing's depiction of transgenerational phenomena, in which the actors change periodically but the characters and plot lines are invariant, seems unlikely as a typical scenario for family life. A typical family script would presumably retain some basic themes and plot lines across generations, but allow the newer actors some room for improvisation in response to changing circumstances and the prompting of their own inner being. Indeed, the measure of a family's health, if I may use that questionable organicist metaphor, resides precisely in its ability to provide such freedom for creative variation while averting the galloping anomie and disintegration that are so common among the Ritalin-riddled households of today.

In any case, while Laing was right to differentiate between his theory and the standard psychoanalytic explanations of transgenerational effects, the fact remains that many aspects of individual temperament really are inherited, and that imitation and identification with one's elders are natural and spontaneous processes. Indeed the attempt to discover or construct a "true" self devoid or divorced from parental "influence" is a perfect chimera. Laing's unwillingness or inability to conceive or concede anything along these lines bespeaks a tendency toward spurious self-creation that the late Charles Rycroft described in his remarkable paper "On the Ablation of Parental Images" (1973).

Though Rycroft's paper only mentions Laing in passing, "On the Ablation of Parental Images" is quite instructive in this regard. Rycroft dismissed Cooper's impossible project of "depopulating" the patient's psyche (Cooper, 1971), and the counterculture's utopian and ahistorical ideal of creating itself and new social relations from scratch. While mindful of the creative possibilities inherent in the mentality of "ablators," as he called them, Rycroft nevertheless insisted that this sort of posture cannot be sustained without well-disguised elements of self-deception and grandiosity. To support this point, he provided numerous clinical illustrations of this process.

Rycroft noted in regard to Laing that his popularity with the young was based on widespread ignorance of how deeply rooted his work was in "establishment" thought, especially the work of Gregory Bateson. While Laing's debt to Bateson can be exaggerated, I thoroughly agree on the more general point. Laing's work was rooted deeply in intellectual traditions that the counterculture had rejected, and as a result, their enthusiasm for him and his ideas was seldom reflected in a substantive understanding of what he was actually saying. Laing was well aware of this. Still, Rycroft's irritation focused on Laing's role as a countercultural icon and should not be construed as a wholesale dismissal. In *A Critical Dictionary of Psychoanalysis,* published five years previously, Rycroft discussed Laing's earlier contributions with sympathy and respect. In the introduction, he wrote:

> The writings of Sartre, R. D. Laing and Rollo May have of recent years aroused considerable interest in the psychotherapeutic professions . . . many of the criticisms and doubts about the validity of basic Freudian assumptions which have been voiced from within the Freudian fold are essentially existential in nature. I refer here to the doubts which have been expressed by Szasz, Home, Lomas, myself and others as to whether the causal-deterministic assumptions of Freudian theory are valid, i.e. whether it is really possible to maintain that human behavior has causes in the sense that physical phenomena do or that human personality can really be explained as a result of events that happened to it as a child . . . existential criticisms of Freudian psychoanalysis are, in general, well informed and made by persons who understand the nature of psychotherapeutic relationships . . . they constitute a greater challenge than do the criticisms of Eysenck and the behavior therapists, which derive from a theoretical position . . . which is concerned to remove the psyche from psychology and attempts to understand human nature by dehumanizing it. (Rycroft, 1968, pp. ix–x)

Unfortunately, during the sixties and seventies few of Laing's fans among the younger generation understood the issues that Rycroft raised here, much less the conceptual intricacies of the double-bind theory. Still, though they lacked the intellectual ballast to fathom his thought, their vivid sense of kinship with Laing was not entirely misguided, as he harbored some of the same "ablating" tendencies as they. Note, for example, his tendency to treat intergenerational transmission as an exclusively *negative* phenomenon (Burston, 1996a, ch. 10). Further evidence of Laing's ablating tendencies can be found in his profound (if problematic) intellectual kinship with Sartre (Kirsner, 1976). As Rycroft pointed out, Sartre's autobiography *The Words* furnishes abundant evidence of schizoid and of ablating tendencies dating back to early childhood. Seen in this light, Sartre's radical voluntarism, his notion of creating oneself from nothing, as it were, suddenly takes on a radically different meaning.

Still, in fairness to Laing—and to Sartre, for that matter—the attempt to trace (real or imagined) intellectual affinities to shared pathognomonic features risks trivializing important issues and fosters an ahistorical approach to the study and discussion of ideas that Rycroft himself deplored. With this caveat in mind, let us recall that despite Sartre's evident appeal to Laing, Laing's appeal to the young in the sixties and seventies was *not* rooted in his Sartrean sensibilities. As Laing himself pointed out (Kirsner in Mullan, 1997), the generation that worshipped him as a guru scarcely read Sartre anymore. And besides, as we've gathered by now, Laing was never a consistent follower of Sartre. I suspect that Laing's former appeal to the young resided in his ability to popularize attitudes characteristic of the Kierkegaardian Christianity in which he had imbibed as a youth, which was wary of collectivism in all its forms, including conventional family piety. Thus, for example, Laing wrote in *Self and Others:* "Jesus spoke of leaving one's parents. Did he mean, among other things, that one is not wise to cling for ultimate security to *their* system of reference, that not this way does one find oneself?" (1961, p. 93). And again, "'I am going to the House of my Lord,' the Christian slave would say, challenged by the Roman soldier. Such equivocation plays upon the inexorable separateness between man and man, that no love, nor the most complete experience of union, completely and permanently annuls" (p. 130).

There are times when these sentiments are entirely appropriate to the situation or stage of life that a person has entered. Even after adolescence has passed, most adults need to re-experience, re-affirm, and express their separateness in various ways. The point is not to get stuck there, to recognize that the movement toward individuation must be followed by an effort to reconnect, to reinsert oneself somehow in the cyclical dance of generations. As Erich Fromm (echoing Buber) pointed out (1964), if the awareness of separateness is not accompanied by renewed resolve and ability to relate authentically, madness and despair are not far off.

Finally, a brief discussion is warranted for one more commonsensical factor affecting the prevailing ignorance and indifference to Laing's family theory. As James Gordon and Elly Jansen point out, many families who have a schizophrenic member do *not* engage in the kind of intensive and all-encompassing mystification, invalidation, and perverse communication that Laing elucidated so cogently in *Sanity, Madness and the Family* (Gordon, 1990; Jansen in Mullan, 1997). In fact, many beleaguered parents would gladly embrace the truth and trade in their illusions and defenses in exchange for the recovery of their loved ones. Moreover, many well-meaning parents who hope to avoid the psychiatric zombification of their offspring consult psychotherapists for insight or interventions for just this purpose, usually in vain. The fact that Laing never acknowledged the existence of these tragic parental dilemmas is not due to faulty methodology but to a lack of generosity and realism, which he regretted in later years.

◆ ◆ ◆

Few would charge Laing with oversimplifying matters. Anyone who actually reads him will appreciate the dense complexity of his ideas. Yet the charge that Laing approached things in a somewhat exaggerated and one-sided fashion has merit and is applicable in a variety of contexts. To reproach someone for one-sidedness, however, is not to dismiss or invalidate him. As Erich Fromm noted with respect to Freud, it is sometimes necessary to exaggerate a point to make it effectively and to draw public attention to phenomena that are likely to be dismissed or ignored otherwise (Fromm, 1980). But Freud succeeded in that regard, at least in the short run. Judging from recent developments, Laing did not. On rare occasions, Laing acknowledged his one-sidedness, but never often or extensively enough to dispel the suspicion that he was just "anti-", or "off the rails"—an impression buttressed by his widespread appeal to the young, whose basic inclinations were anti-intellectual. Still, when purged of polemical excess and taken with a salutary grain of salt, Laing's reflections on the nature, origins, and meaning of family difficulties are as relevant now as they ever were—not to all families, but to many. Let us hope they get a proper hearing.

NORMALITY AND
THE NUMINOUS

$\cdots \Big|\; 5 \;\Big| \cdots$

Recent studies using the revised third edition of *Diagnostic and Statistical Manual of Mental Disorders* suggest that more than 25 percent of the adult population of the United States will suffer from a severe mental illness this year, while another 60 percent are expected to suffer symptoms of mild to moderate severity at some time in their lives. The inference is straightforward. By prevailing standards, less than 15 percent of the adult population is presently expected to enjoy continuous, uninterrupted, and vibrant mental health during their lifetimes. In short, normality isn't normal anymore—if indeed, it ever was (Kirk and Kutchins, 1992; Caplan, 1995).

Given the prevalence of mental disorder as it is currently defined, the tacit equation between "health" and "normality," while convenient in view of common usage, does not really hold up under scrutiny. Yet this promiscuous and illogical usage persists universally. As a result, there is a great deal of unconscious confusion about, which is attributable to the fact that there are not one, but really *four* concepts of normality currently in vogue: the statistical, the cultural, the medical, and the psychopathological.

Taken on its own terms, the statistical model of normality is the most simple and straightforward. What is "normal" in any given setting is the central tendency or prevailing trend, which varies according to what you are measuring. Thus, for example, if the life span of the average male in the former Soviet Union has dropped from age seventy to age sixty since perestroika, then death at sixty is the new norm. However much we may deplore this trend, humanly speaking, the fact remains that a statistical norm has no intrinsic moral or political significance, even though it can be used (or misused) for political or moral ends. Why? Because statistical data do not *prescribe* anything. They merely *describe* an existing state of affairs without applying any (intrinsic or extrinsic) scale of values to them. In short, they are—or ought to be—purely descriptive, value neutral, and context dependent.

The cultural concept of normality is also context dependent and varies from one society to another. But unlike the statistical approach, it is overtly *prescriptive* and entails standards of conduct and belief, deviance from which is deemed bad or mad. Moral and political issues, and judgments regarding age- and gender-appropriate behavior, which are irrelevant to the statistical model, are central here because the cultural concept of normality measures any given state of affairs against an "ought" that is taken to be self-evident or uncontroversial. So if a teenager engages in premarital sex in a culture where such activity is frowned upon, she risks censure regardless of the actual frequency of this occurrence. Unlike the statistical model, the cultural concept of normality is overtly (or implicitly) prescriptive, but like it, is intrinsically context dependent, even when it aspires to legislate norms that are binding on all humanity and for all time.

The medical concept of normality is more ambiguous than the preceding two, because it contains both descriptive and prescriptive elements and dimensions of relativity and universality that are commingled in various complicated ways. As the late Peter Sedgwick pointed out (1982), there is nothing "unnatural" or anomalous about diseases. As far as nature is concerned, they are not genuine aberrations, but population control devices. It is *we* who attach a negative value to them and a positive value to "health." To that extent, diseases are social constructions, and prescriptive ones at that.

Our criteria of physical health and illness are not merely prescriptive, however. They are also *descriptive,* and allowing for regional and/or genetic variations, apply (with minor qualifications) to all human beings, regardless of cultural or historical context. Take the following statements: "The more one engages in promiscuous sex, the greater one's risk of acquiring a sexually transmitted disease, including HIV. The risk is even greater if one does not engage in protected or 'safe sex.'" On the face of it, these statements contain no moralizing. They are empirical generalizations rooted in experience. Nevertheless, cautionary statements like these entail the assumption that disease is bad, even if the behavior that leads to it is not. The medical concept of normality is therefore partly descriptive, partly prescriptive, inherently value laden, and actually or incipiently universal in character, despite important regional and/or age- and sex-based variations in what constitutes "normal" functioning.

Historically, the psychopathological concept of normality is an offshoot of the medical model. It posits universal norms of psychological functioning and/or relatedness to others according to which any individual may be judged disturbed, disordered, or well. Like the medical model, it is value laden and aspires to universality. But while the human body may be measured and studied by natural scientific methods, the "psyche" is an elusive entity that cannot be studied apart from the macro- and micro social contexts in which "it" is embedded. There is even legitimate disagreement about whether or not there is actually a discrete entity—a "psyche"—in which the alleged "pathology" resides, and whether the processes deemed pathological according to psychopathological criteria are even truly "interior" to the patient, or (as Laing contended) merely a personal response to the real locus of disturbance in the patient's interpersonal, familial, or social surroundings.

Like the medical model, the psychopathological approach is partly descriptive and partly prescriptive. But the fusion or confusion of descriptive and prescriptive levels of analysis here may cause more mischief than it does in the medical model. As I noted previously, many judgments about the conduct and beliefs of patients using psychopathological criteria are heavily influenced by social and cultural biases that shape the "psyches" of practitioners unawares (Caplan, 1995; Kirschner, 1996). Moreover, these judgments are routinely disguised as purely descriptive or value free, when they are inherently prescriptive in character. Laing was quite sensitive to problems like these. His father, David Laing, was a deep (if unconventional) believer who saw an angel when he was fourteen. Though he was lying in bed at the time, he claimed to be completely lucid and awake during this brief but transforming experience. The suspicion that this is evidence of latent psychotic trends entails the prescriptive assertion that Laing's father ought *not* to have seen an angel: that such an event, being rare, is pathological. Laing resented this sort of inference, not least because it trivializes religious experience.

On reflection, then, it transpires that the meanings, measures, and morals attached to these four models of normality often overlap. This is particularly true in stable societies, where a strong cultural consensus prevails. In instances like these, statistical norms describing predominant patterns of behavior and belief tend to coincide with cultural norms. When this is the case, these norms are often accorded a specious universality that they do not deserve, except in the cultural imagination. When this is not the case, we have curious but pervasive inconsistencies between theory and practice, as in the case of American Catholics, the majority of whom use birth control despite the condemnation of their church. Here a palpable rift exists between cultural and statistical norms, albeit in a stable configuration.

At other times—for example, during periods of social upheaval or mass immigration—statistical and cultural norms diverge so widely and/or change so rapidly that a cultural consensus or central tendency may even be difficult to discern. Take the norm of the two-parent nuclear family. Most of us pay it lip service, yet the gap between cultural theory and practice grows steadily, and if current trends prevail, one-parent families will soon become the statistical norm. Where cultural norms and common practice diverge, the term "normality" loses its seeming self-evidence and transparency. Instead it becomes a loaded expression that either conveys or conceals a social or political agenda that has nothing to do with simple empirical truth.

So despite some harmonious possibilities in ideal circumstances, the four concepts of normality do not always converge or complement one another. In fact, they are often at variance. Yet when people use the word "normal" to describe a particular kind of experience, expression, or belief, they are usually operating under the naive misimpression that (1) they really know what the word normal means, and (2) that others understand their words in the same way they do. Unfortunately, however, our concepts of normality are often subtly confused and confusing in ways that we are simply not aware of. And in any given situation, our assertion about a particular item or category of "normal" experience or behavior—

yours, mine, or theirs—may strike our interlocutors in a very different way than we intend, whether or not we (or they) are aware of it.

Unfortunately, laymen and professionals alike prefer to ignore this veritable confusion of tongues, and are tacitly encouraged to do so by the mental health authorities. Witness the successive editions of the *Diagnostic and Statistical Manual of Mental Disorders,* published by the American Psychiatric Association, which attempts to describe and classify mental "illnesses" in the manifest absence of both a clear definition of mental health and any consideration of whether (or in what circumstances) mental health and statistical normality actually coincide, or even *can* coincide. This approach ignores the essential circularity and complementarity of our ideas about mental health and mental disorder. To say that something is abnormal presupposes an implicit notion of normality and therefore begs the question as to *which* concept of normality is being invoked or expressed, if only indirectly. Analogously, to say that something is morbid or unhealthy presupposes a norm of health that may or may not be universally binding, or even relevant to the nature and source of the patient's real difficulty.

As a rule, mental health professionals are far too pragmatic and problem-focused to trouble themselves with problems of this nature or magnitude. So when they do get around to defining normality, it is usually one-dimensionally, as a conflict-free adaptation to one's surroundings and/or as the absence of overt symptomatology. As I will describe later, Laing railed against this tendency, often adding that current diagnostic schemata are frequently vaguely worded and overly-inclusive—that almost anything can count as a symptom of certain disorders. Along with many others, I share Laing's misgivings on this point and think that women, children, and minorities are overrepresented in many categories of mental disorder. Certain categories that presumably apply to them alone seem instead to disguise complex social, economic, and cultural problems that we prefer not to face forthrightly (Chesler, 1975; Mirowsky and Ross, 1989; Brown, 1990; Cohen, 1990; Kirk and Kutchins, 1992; Breggin, 1991; Caplan, 1995; Armstrong, 1997).

Valid as these arguments are, however, the point I am making is a slightly different one. Even if the criteria and boundaries of these diagnostic criteria were *not* exceedingly nebulous in many cases, the fact remains that at a basic, conceptual level, mental health professionals never elucidate the various meanings of normality or separate the descriptive and prescriptive levels of analysis within one and the same approach. If they did, the aura of self-evidence that attaches to the term "normality" would vanish, and all kinds of troubling questions would emerge.

Occasionally, the better minds in the mental health field acknowledge, or at least hint at, these underlying problems. For example, many of the authors of the fourth edition of the *Diagnostic and Statistical Manual* freely concede that the boundaries between a disorder and a "non-disorder" are often blurry. But what these boundaries lack in conceptual sophistication or historical awareness, they claim, they make up for in practical utility. Perhaps. A facile definition of normality in terms of adjustment or mere freedom from symptoms is certainly convenient for any discipline that seeks to normalize a patient's behavior and utterances without reflecting too long or too deeply on the nature of its commitment. But what if, in good skeptical fashion, we assume that the opposite is true, and explore the possibilities that open up? In other words, what if we assume that normality and mental health are not *necessarily* identical, and that the absence of experienced conflict is an indication not of genuine sanity, but of bland indifference, a want of realism and sensitivity, and negative capability?

In effect, Laing did just that. By contrast with the majority of his colleagues, Laing construed normality as a kind of deficiency disease—one characterized by a lack of authenticity and/or access to the deeper levels of the psyche (that is, the primitive and the sublime), which are integral to the wholeness of human experience. This attitude perplexes laymen and professionals alike. For cultural and historical reasons, we Westerners habitually construe madness in privative terms, as the *loss* of reason, of ego functions, relatedness to others, and so forth, and regard normality as a state of plenitude, or of robust benefits (virtues?) that no reasonable person would ever wish to discard. But if Laing is correct, the reverse is often true—normality entails hidden losses, while madness may harbor potential benefits, if we have the patience and insight to bring them to fruition.

Laing's critique of normality unfolded in several stages, beginning with *The Divided Self* and culminating in *The Politics of Experience* and *The Politics of the Family*. In *The Divided Self*, he noted that the "normal" individual is someone who enjoys a relatively stable and continuous sense of identity, a feeling of personal autonomy and of being comfortable with his or her body, and above all, an ability for authentic self-disclosure emanating from a state of *primary ontological security*. While Laing made normality sound quite attractive by comparison with the wretchedness and despair of schizoid and schizophrenic experience, he did not glamorize it the way most of his contemporaries in the mental health field did. Like Martin Buber, Laing suggested that most relationships between normal people are driven or at least colored by various personal or impersonal-bureaucratic agendas that preclude authentic meeting with others because they reduce the person before us to the status of an instrument, a thing, rather than evoking an I-Thou dialectic of mutual recognition. In chapter 3 of *The Divided Self,* for example, Laing noted that "a partial depersonalization of others is extensively practiced in everyday life and is regarded as normal if not highly desirable. Most relationships are based on some partial depersonalizing tendency in so far as one treats the other not in terms of any awareness of who or what he might be in himself but as virtually an android robot playing or acting a role or part in a large machine in which one too may be acting" (Laing, 1960, p. 47).

Nevertheless, Laing observed somewhat later:

> In the "normal" person a good number of his actions may be virtually mechanical. These areas of virtually mechanical behavior do not, however, necessarily encroach on every aspect of everything he does, they do not absolutely preclude the emergence of spontaneous expressions, and they are not so completely against the grain that the individual seeks actively to repudiate them as foreign bodies lodged in his make-up. Moreover, they do not assume an autonomous compulsive way of their own, such that the individual feels that they are living or rather killing him, rather than he living them. The issue, at any rate, does not arise with such painful intensity that he must attack or destroy this alien reality within himself as though it had an almost separate (personal) existence. (Laing, 1960, p. 95)

In *Self and Others,* published in 1961, Laing's definition of normality shifted significantly. Formerly, Laing had described normality in terms of a stable sense of identity, a capacity for self-disclosure and relatedness, an identification with one's body, and so on, but had qualified his characterization with sobering reminders about the prevalence of reification in contemporary life. Now, however, Laing defined normality as a state of unconscious complicity in "social phantasy systems." Though he never actually defined this term, its derivation and uses suggest that at the macrosocial level, social phantasy systems include religious creeds, political ideologies, and a dull, unreflective scientism—all of which shape one's world view, but whose manifest irrationality does not provoke skepticism or disbelief among true believers. And on the microsocial level, social phantasy systems include a startlingly diverse range of family mythologies and organizational myths and metaphors.

Interestingly, this equivocal conjunction of sanity and insanity is a vivid characterization of many racists, religious fanatics, and ultranationalists of all shades and denominations. People like this may appear relatively sane in terms of their image of and attitude toward their bodies, as well as their capacity for relationships *within* their own reference group, but they are utterly blind and irrational where outsiders are at issue. This is supposedly common knowledge. Curiously, however, Laing thought that this equivocal condition was not merely the domain of bigots, cranks, and extremists, but of almost everyone. In his own words, "The normal state of affairs is to be so immersed in one's immersion in social phantasy systems that one takes them to be real" (Laing, 1961, p. 38).

This argument is repeated with even greater emphasis in *The Politics of Experience*, where Laing declared, "The tremendous social realities of our time are ghosts, specters of murdered gods and our own humanity returned to haunt us . . . the fabric of these socially shared hallucinations is what we call reality, and our collusive madness is what we call sanity" (Laing, 1967, p. 73).

Instead of stressing the advantages of normality, as he did in *The Divided Self*, in *The Politics of Experience* Laing reversed his initial emphasis and stressed what is lost to repression. What is repressed among normal people, explained Laing, are not merely instincts (Freud), nor the memory of specific events or losses and the feelings and phantasies engendered by them, but whole modalities and possibilities of experience and relatedness to others that are proscribed by society as irrational, excessive, infantile, and so on. The awareness of the tragic, the sublime, the absurd, the prevalence and persistence of evil, and the peace that passeth understanding—these innately human sensibilities are severely stunted, if not extinguished, in the struggle to adapt to contemporary society. Indeed these play very muted and transient roles in our lives, instead of occupying center stage, as Laing evidently felt they should. Yet the self-estrangement inherent in this process is not a source of consciously experienced suffering, nor of unconscious conflict (neurosis à la Freud). On the contrary, this atrophy of the spirit *dissipates* conflict, leading to a conflict-free adaptation to one's surroundings—one that passes for health, more or less.

As I noted in *The Wing of Madness,* Laing's withering appraisal of normality shaped his attitude toward socialization as well. By his reckoning, families, schools, and churches provide us with little more than a systematic training in self-estrangement and inauthenticity—a secular equivalent to the Fall. Just as striking, in retrospect, is how often and how earnestly Laing disparaged normality with religious tropes and metaphors. For example, in *The Politics of Experience,* he writes: "We are all fallen Sons of Prophecy, who have learned to die in the Spirit and be reborn in the Flesh" (Laing, 1967, p. 68). And again later: "There is a prophecy in Amos that a time will come when there will be a famine in the land, 'not a famine for bread, nor a thirst for water, but of *hearing* the words of the Lord.' That time has now come to pass. It is the present age" (p. 144).

Laing held that the pseudo-sanity of the normal person entails a progressive attentuation of authenticity, which erodes his or her critical faculty and openness to transcendental experience. True sanity, he said, involves the dissolution of the normally adjusted ego, which he equated with the false self, in a process that, following Jung, he termed "metanoia." The transcendence of the ego can be sought deliberately through meditation and spiritual practices, which provide useful templates for interpreting and managing the troubling and disruptive inner tumult that is bound to occur along the way. Or such transcendence can occur spontaneously. The mad person, by Laing's reckoning, has been catapulted into this process unawares and without skillful guidance will go astray—that is, will be exiled indefinitely to the demonic realms of the mind that enshroud and obstruct our access to the holy. So the therapist becomes a spiritual midwife, even a shaman of sorts, while his distressed and dissociated patient becomes a "hierophant of the sacred."

Laing's approach to madness, and his attempt to link it with transcendental experience, was one source of his fame and notoriety. But we are interested in his attitudes toward "normal" people, not the mad. So it is interesting to note that the absence or atrophy of the numinous that Laing associated with normalization in the modern, secular world was linked—in his mind, anyway—with the problem of violence. In *The Politics of Experience,* published in 1967, Laing noted that allegedly normal men had killed approximately 100 million of their own kind in the preceding fifty years—a rate of slaughter unprecedented, indeed unimaginable, in any other century. Moreover, said Laing, the escalating scale and widening scope of violence in our time is not the result of innate propensities to violence and indiscipline—a "death instinct," as Freud believed —but was caused by deep psychic damage wrought by the effort to adapt to an irrational world bereft of transcendence. Without saying so in so many words, Laing therefore implied that there is a strong correlation between the progressive secularization of society and the proliferation of evil in everyday life.

On the face of it, this claim could gladden the heart of any religious conservative or New Age enthusiast. And it is true that many took offense at Laing's religious imagery and said that his prophetic airs ill suited a man of science. Still, in fairness to Laing, he did not actually claim that increasing secularization *causes* increased violence. That would have put him in the same company as Girolamo Savonarolla, Joseph de Maistre, and the Ayatollah Khomeini. It would also have put him in opposition to the whole Enlightenment tradition that welcomed secularization as a necessary prelude to general human emancipation. Though he was wary of Enlightenment rationalism, like any good existentialist, that was just not his style.

No, Laing's approach to transcendental experience was a bit more complicated than that. Laing argued, in effect, that the violence we do to ourselves in the process of normalization is reflected, among other things, in the decline of the numinous as a dimension of normal human experience. Interpersonal and collective violence is but one more symptom of the same underlying malaise. Much as he lamented the loss of the numinous, however, Laing was not advocating a return to a repressive, theocratic society, nor to a religious creed based on a dogmatic interpretation of scriptures. In fact, like Jung, Laing was apt to disparage religious belief as a poor and inauthentic substitute for religious experience. As he writes in *The Politics of Experience* (1967):

> Nowhere in the Bible is there any argument about the *existence* of gods, demons, angels. People did not first "believe in" God: they experienced His presence, as was true of other spiritual agencies. The question was not whether God existed, but whether this particular God was the greatest god of all, or the only God; and what was the relation of the various spiritual agencies to one another. Today, there is public debate, not as to the trustworthiness of God, the particular place in the spiritual hierarchy of different spirits, but whether God or such spirits *even exist* or ever have existed. (pp. 140–141)

> Faith was never a matter of believing He existed, but of trusting in the presence that was experienced and known to exist as a self-validating datum. (p. 142)

> Many people are prepared to have faith in the sense of a scientifically indefensible belief in an untested hypothesis. Few have enough trust to test it. (pp. 142–143)

> We live in a secular world. To adapt to this world the child abdicates its ecstasy. ("L'enfant abdique son ecstase": Mallarmé). Having lost our experience of the spirit, we are expected to have faith. (p. 144)

Though seldom mentioned in *The Politics of Experience,* the parallels to Jung are extensive and profound. Jung carefully distinguished between a creed (or faith)—a system of belief adhered to rigidly and uncritically in the absence of compelling proof that draws its authority from consensus and tradition—and the self-authorizing, self-validating transcendental experience that presumably underlies all religious symbols (Jung, 1933; 1935; 1964). On the whole, Jung was a little more diplomatic than Laing in his characterization of religious creeds, but he just as avidly sought direct knowledge and religious experience. The difference between them was that Jung's Gnostic affinities were overtly and articulately affirmed and expressed (Segal, 1992), while Laing's were merely hinted at. Nevertheless, the Gnostic thread is unmistakable, and evidenced in a footnote to chapter 4 of *The Divided Self,* where Laing notes the resemblance between the schizoid patient's pursuit of disembodied selfhood and the Gnostic's disincarnate spirituality. It is apparent as well in *Self and Others,* chapter 2, where Laing invokes Gnostic imagery to describe the common run of humanity: that we are dead, but think we are alive; asleep, but think we are awake; mad, but have no insight, and so forth (1961, p. 38). Finally, it is evident both in *The Bird of Paradise,* which opens with a quote from the Gnostic *Gospel of Thomas,* and in the intense preoccupation he shared with Gregory Bateson in 1968 regarding the Gnostic ideas of *Pleroma* and *Creatura,* which figured strongly in Jung's work as well.

Laing's affinities with (and indebtedness to) Jung become even more obvious when he details the nature and extent of our collective alienation from the "inner" world and condemns the ego as an agent of adaptation to "external" reality, equating it with the "false self." Though he never said so succinctly, the Freudian view of the ego evoked his contempt because of the premium it placed on adapting to reality, relinquishing phantasy, and so on; in this way, he felt, it devalued contact with the realms of reverie and contemplation that earlier civilizations had cultivated carefully. By Laing's reckoning, our radical estrangement from phantasy and "inner" experience is just as detrimental to our sanity, in the long run, as the psychotic's estrangement from the external world around him.

While indebted to Jung in many respects, Laing's critique of normality in *The Politics of Experience* also leaned on another modern Gnostic, namely Martin Heidegger. Unlike Jung, Heidegger was not preoccupied with the psychology of religion or transcendental experience per se. But like Kierkegaard, Heidegger was intensely concerned with the problem of authenticity, and by implication, thought Laing, with the problem of alienation. As Laing wrote in the introduction to *The Politics of Experience* (1967), "Our alienation goes to the roots. The realization of this is the essential springboard for any serious reflection on any aspect of present interhuman life. Viewed from different perspectives, construed in different ways and expressed in different idioms, this realization unites men as diverse as Marx, Kierkegaard, Nietzsche, Freud, Heidegger, Tillich and Sartre" (Laing, 1967, introduction).

Many philosophers would dispute Laing's contention that Heidegger was really concerned with alienation, at least in the technical, Marxist sense. And perhaps he was not. But Heidegger's concepts of inauthenticity and of the "homelessness" of modern man do bear a resemblance to Marx's ideas on self-estrangement, as Heidegger himself acknowledged. In a famous letter to Jean

Beaufret, Heidegger wrote, "What Marx, on the basis of Hegel's philosophy, recognized in an essential and important sense of as man's alienation, has its roots in the homelessness of modern man ... Since Marx, in his awareness of this alienation, attains an essential dimension of history, the Marxist conception of history is superior to all others" (Friedman, 1994, p. 262).

Heidegger's praise for Hegel and Marx was odd, to say the least, because he addressed the issue of self-estrangement from a completely different angle. To say, as Laing did, that Heidegger and Marx were addressing the same problem but from different perspectives and in different idioms, may simplify matters considerably, but it just does not do justice to the subtle but profound tensions between these two protean thinkers. To get their differences into historical and theoretical perspective, remember that alienation, in the first instance, connotes a state or process whereby one becomes separated or estranged from one's original condition, hopefully as a prelude to a subsequent return to it. For example, in Heraclitus, and according to Stoicism and neo-Platonism, one is alienated from the Absolute until death, when the divine spark entrapped in our mundane body returns to the One, the World Soul or Primal Fire. Or in Christian theology, alienation from God through the Fall (original sin) is remedied by repentance, faith, and good works, which promote reconciliation with the Deity (Abrams, 1971).

Ancient concepts of alienation were invariably cast in philosophical or religious terms and percolated through the collective consciousness of Western man in the form of Christian neo-Platonism and negative theology. Hegel, who was well versed in these traditions, gave the term alienation a new and more specific meaning linked to his philosophy of history. Hegel construed human history as a process wherein God—or Absolute Spirit—loses and gradually recovers Itself, using successive phases of human civilization as way stations on the path to self-knowledge. Initially, Absolute Spirit, as the ground of Being, exists "in itself" in a primordial and undifferentiated state of nature. To become "for-itself"—that is, self-conscious—Absolute Spirit has to externalize and objectify itself in the natural and historical worlds, and therefore through man, whose various faiths and philosophies attest to successive stages in the evolving self-consciousness of the Deity (Fackenheim, 1970).

By contrast with Hegel, who retained a religious dimension in his concept of alienation, Marx secularized it completely. Marx construed Hegel's depiction of the alienation and self-recovery of Absolute Spirit as a mystified account of a specifically human process—the estrangement of men and women from themselves, from the species, and from nature. This estrangement is due to the way their own labor or productivity (and its resultant artifacts) become alienated from them as labor becomes increasingly mechanized, specialized, and commodified, and as reification subsumes more and more of the social and interpersonal worlds. But despite his critique of Hegel's religiosity, Marx also saw history as a (more or less) cumulative, linear progression in which alienation would ultimately be transcended—not merely in consciousness, but practically, in a society free of exploitation and oppression.

As many critics (such as Fromm, 1961) have observed, Marx's theory of a postrevolutionary social order is really a secularization of the Messianic Age. Moreover, Marx's prophetic concern with justice for the downtrodden and dispossessed imparted a unique pathos to his work, whereas for Hegel self-knowledge was paramount (Rockmore, 1997). But unlike Hegel and Marx, Heidegger did *not* conceive of human history as a cumulative, unified, and linear process resulting in Absolute Knowledge or in general human emancipation. Nor did Heidegger think of human history as a process of collective self-creation or self-authorship. Like all existentialists, beginning with Kierkegaard, Heidegger conceived of self-creation, self-authorship, and so on as the result of individual choices and decisions.

Heidegger's concept of alienation, if that is what it is, was articulated in *Being and Time* (1927). Heidegger thought of self-estrangement in terms of our immersion in *das Mann* or the "public world," which is characterized by ambiguity, idle talk, and curiosity. Briefly, idle talk is pseudo-communication, where the participants do not stand in any meaningful relation to one another and/or to the subject of their conversation. This leads to superficiality of discourse—speaking for the sake of speaking or being spoken to, regardless of whether or not one has anything meaningful to say. Curiosity is a need for distraction, novelty, or stimulation—a degraded substitute of the capacity for genuine wonder. In both instances, Heidegger says, specifically human capacities are stunted or deformed.

But when *Dasein*, or the distinctively human way of "being-in-the-world," shuts out the "noise" of the world, it experiences a state of *unheimlichkeit* (the uncanny), in which it is freed to experience its own inner nature as "thrown." As Heidegger writes on p. 323 of *Being and Time*: "Uncanniness is the basic kind of Being-in-the-world, even though in an everyday way it has been covered up." And again, on p. 333, "In uncanniness, Dasein stands together with itself primordially."

In view of common usage, Heidegger's notion of self-estrangement and his linkage of authenticity to *Unheimlichkeit* strike many people as counterintuitive. When you or I talk of feeling "alienated" from someone or something, we usually mean that we feel distinctly ill at ease in its presence, or somehow deeply at variance with its way of being. When a sense of estrangement from others crops up in *Being and Time,* however, Heidegger invariably puts a *positive* spin on it, because he regarded alienation from the public world as a prelude to authentic self-recovery. By his reckoning, the sense of being "at home" or comfortable in the public world is really a symptom of the numbing of our authentic inner voice.

According to Heidegger, the uncanniness that *Dasein* experiences when released to experience its own possibilities occurs only when the self is deeply attuned to itself *(Befindlichkeit),* to its essential throwness *(Geworfenheit)* and possibility *(Möglichkeit).* In his own words:

In conscience *Dasein* calls itself. (p. 320)

The caller is unfamiliar to the everyday they-self; it is something like an alien voice. What could be more alien to the "they," lost in the manifold world of its concern, than the Self which has been individualized down to itself in uncanniness and been thrown into the "nothing"? (pp. 321–322)

The call of conscience, existentially understood, makes known for the first time what we have hitherto merely contended: that uncanniness pursues Dasein and is a threat to the lostness in which it has forgotten itself. (p. 322)

To restate this idea in ordinary English, the fact that conscience emerges as an "alien voice" is a symptom of our "fallenness" or self-alienation. Moreover, a sense of deepening estrangement from the public world—the "they"—heralds growing self-knowledge and self-awareness, and absent the requisite estrangement from others, genuine self-knowledge cannot be achieved. Or to revert again to Heidegger's idiom, we might say that by active absorption in others—a process called "eddying" in Joan Staumbaugh's recent translation of *Being and Time*—*Dasein* inevitably lapses or falls into inauthenticity, or a denial/unawareness of its own contingency and above all, its finitude and eventual death.

That being so, the recovery and/or preservation of authenticity is an ongoing project for the resolute individual and is inextricably tied up with his or her awareness of death. But nothing in Heidegger suggests that any kind of radical reform or social transformation can alter the terms of the self and its dispersal in (and recovery from) "the *they.*" This is a critical divergence from Marx. In Marx's *Economic and Philosophic Manuscripts,* alienation from self and alienation from others go hand in hand. They are inextricably interwoven, so to mitigate or abolish the one, you have to address the other simultaneously (Fromm, 1961). By contrast, Heidegger implies that being deeply attuned to oneself and being in such harmony with others are mutually antagonistic states. In his own words, "Dasein, as a being-with which understands, can listen to the Others. Losing itself in the publicness and idle talk of the 'they,' it fails to hear its ownself in listening to the they-self. If Dasein is able to get brought back from this lostness of failing to hear itself, and if this is to be done through itself, then it must first be able to find itself—to find itself as something which has failed to hear itself, and which fails to hear in that it *listens away* to the they. This *listening away* must get broken off."

In 1952, Hans Jonas first called attention to the Gnostic tropes in *Being and Time.* The theme of an alien voice recalling the individual from his lostness or dispersal in the collective false-consciousness is one. And so indeed are the suggestions that the sense of dread, of the uncanny, are a prelude to or corollary of the soul's discovery of its basic situation, and that the general run of humanity tries to avoid or evade an authentic self-awareness by immersion in the *lethe* (oblivion of the crowd). Finally, there is the antinomian thread in Heidegger's discussion of conscience, where he opposes the authentic conscience of the individual with his inauthentic (public) conscience. Like the Gnostics, and like Nietzsche, Heidegger felt that the epistemic elite, those truly "in the know," are not bound by the same moral precepts that govern the rest of us. They are answerable to themselves alone (Jonas, 1963; 1974).

Evidence of Heidegger's influence on Laing is both direct and indirect. As noted previously, the first tangible indication is the discussion of existential guilt in *The Divided Self,* chapter 8, which we pondered previously. Another appears in *Self and Others,* where Laing invoked Heidegger's concept of truth as *aletheia,* or uncovering, from the latter's then as yet untranslated book on *Parmenides* (Laing, 1961, p. 129; Heidegger, 1982). And elsewhere in *Self and Others,* Laing argued that normal individuals are enmeshed in social phantasy systems that alienate them from their own experience. Without invoking Heidegger by name, Laing described the individual who is emancipating from the they-self as engaged in a process of "derealization" that briefly shatters his or her mental equilibrium, but both alerts them to their lostness or dispersal in *das Mann* and awakens them to their own authentic selfhood.

Yet another indication of Heidegger's influence on Laing is found in *The Politics of Experience,* chapter 5. Here Laing asks us to imagine a group of airplanes in flight where one pilot strays deliberately from the rest of the formation. In the eyes of the other pilots, this one is "abnormal" or "deviant" even if the formation as a whole is unwittingly off course. Analogously, said Laing, the clinical criterion of health or sanity is whether or not the individual is acting in concert with the judgments and perceptions of his peers, regardless of whether or to what extent their *collective* judgment is impaired. And he warned us not to assume that because a group is "in formation" they are necessarily "on course." From the ontological standpoint, said Laing, the abnormal one's orientation may actually be more congruent with reality.

Though he did not spell them out, the implications for therapy of this train of thought are intriguing. Evidently, said Laing, there is no need to idealize someone who is "out of formation" (that is, deviant) because there is no guarantee that this individual is actually "on course," or closer to existential actualities than the majority of their peers. But by the same token, it is misguided to persuade someone who is "out of formation" that a "cure" consists in normalization, or getting back "in formation." In fact, if the majority are unwittingly off course, then the only way to get back on course is to deviate from them (Laing, 1967, pp. 118–120).

As Michael Thompson points out, this is a Heideggerian proverb in which the mindless crowd seeks to reabsorb the reticent individual—who is called to reverie and solitude—and attempts to substitute their ambiguity and idle chatter for his authentically grounded way of being. Leaning on Heidegger, Laing was saying in effect that statistical and/or cultural normality are not guarantees of sound judgment or genuine sanity. From the standpoint of an "ideal observer," or from the "ontological standpoint," the compact majority may be deviating as far (or farther) from the true path as the allegedly abnormal individual. Admittedly, Laing did not invoke Heidegger explicitly here. But he did make references throughout *The Politics of Experience* to the alienated individual recovering or rediscovering the "inner light." This phrase, borrowed from Christian mysticism, allusively conjures up Heidegger's concept of conscience, as well as related ideas about the "inner light" from Sufism, Buddhism, and elsewhere.

The question then emerges: is Heidegger's theory of self-estrangement and authenticity tenable? Yes and no, but certainly no more than its Marxist precursor. Admittedly, Heidegger's approach to the modern malaise is free of the progressivist historicism of Hegel and Marx. But what it gained in historical objectivity, it lost in its utter disregard for the manifold deformations of sociability engendered by the vicissitudes of work in an exploitative and class-structured society (Burston, 1996b). Moreover, despite copious disclaimers to the contrary, Heidegger's depiction of the self's recovery from its fragmentation and dispersion in "the they" pits the solitary individual against a corrupting society with the same pathos that we find in Jean-Jacques Rousseau—or Ayn Rand, for that matter. Thus there are subtle contradictions between Heidegger's ostensibly non-dualist ontology and his concept of conscience, which as Martin Buber discerned, harbors strong strains of individualism, albeit in highly mystified form.

Moreover, it is interesting to note that while Marx celebrated *praxis* and productivity (Fromm, 1961), Heidegger harbored a deep distrust of human agency, embodied in his enigmatic "Will-not-to-will." The meaning of this phrase, and its bearing on his work as a whole, is a still matter of controversy, however. In *The Life of the Mind* (1971), Hannah Arendt construed it as being emblematic of *die Kehre*—the "reversal" or "turning" that Heidegger underwent circa 1936–1940, when he was composing his two volumes on Nietzsche. On Arendt's reading, Heidegger's Will-not-to-will is a repudiation of (1) Nietzsche's "will to power," which Heidegger interpreted as a preeminently destructive force, and (2) his own involvement with the Nazis some years previously (pp. 172–174).

Some will dispute the accuracy of my characterization and will cite the shift that the term *Sorge*—care—undergoes after Heidegger's *die Kehre* to refute the contention that he distrusted human agency. In *Being and Time,* they might argue, *Sorge* denoted a lively apprehension or vigilance on behalf of oneself and/or those to whom one is closely attached, a feeling often (though inadequately) translated as "anxiety." Thus Arendt. (Others, like Hans Jonas, construe *Sorge* as a synonym for will.) But later, Arendt contends (1971, p. 183), *Sorge* denotes an active devotion to the preservation of Being, rather than an essentially *self-preservative* impulse. On this later reading, apparently, the uniquely attuned and responsive person is described variously as a "guardian," "servant," or "shepherd" of Being, ever on the alert for encroaching threats, ever ready to witness, facilitate, or lend a hand.

Granted. Still, if we take these metaphors to heart, the fact remains that the kind of activeness at issue here is really more *reactive* and *conservative* in character. It is roused to activity from an attentive (but nonetheless passive) communion as circumstances require. It does not initiate, interrogate, transform, or create on its own behalf. Nor does it seek self-fulfillment or self-expression in the creative act. It simply watches and protects, and is "obedient" to Being. If it diverges from this path, presumably it embodies or at any rate sanctions an illegitimate drive to domination.[1]

In any case, no matter how we construe Heidegger on the subject of human agency, the fact remains that any interpretation we embrace must hinge to some extent on how we construe *die Kehre.* Heidegger drew public attention to *die Kehre* in his famous 1949 "Letter" to Jean Beaufret and attached much importance to it. But a curious feature of *die Kehre* that Arendt (and others) overlook is that during World War II, most of Heidegger's contemporaries interpreted it as a conciliatory move *toward* Nazism, rather than away from it (Bronner, 1994, p. 107). Furthermore, *die Kehre* entailed the methodical elimination of non-German and non-Greek terminology from his work. This goal was inspired by the conviction that Greek and German are kindred languages and are intrinsically "in tune" with Being, whereas philosophical terminology derived from Latin and the Romance languages foster *Seinsvergessenheit*—

forgetfulness of Being. Whatever motivated this linguistic shift in Heidegger it is intriguing to note that it coincided with Hitler's attempt to purify vernacular German of all foreign words and influences, and to reintroduce the old Gothic script for purposes of everyday communication (Bronner, 1994).

In any case, in Arendt's view, Heidegger's concurrent rejection of Nietzsche and the Nazis entailed the assumption that the Nazis were acting according to a Nietzschean philosophy—or that Heidegger thought so, anyway. And in fairness to Heidegger (if that is what he thought), there are many instances where Nietzsche confused and conflated the ideas of activeness and aggression, and where Hitler clumsily paraphrased Nietzsche, so one can see why Heidegger may have arrived at this conclusion. In view of Laing's many debts to Heidegger, however, note that he did *not* interpret Nietzsche this way (for example, Laing, 1961, p. 127), nor was he mistrustful of human agency generally. Indeed, agency is central to Laing's view of personhood, and by his own admission, he was deeply influenced by the Scottish philosopher John MacMurray, author of *Self as Agent* (1957).[2]

Nevertheless, in *The Politics of Experience,* Laing adopted a somewhat Heideggerian tone regarding creativity. Remember that in addition to being mistrustful of human agency, the later Heidegger was very wary of humanism. Indeed, as his letter to Beaufret suggests, the later Heidegger saw humanism as an anthropocentric distortion of existential ontology. Nevertheless, even the later Heidegger allowed that humans have a distinctive way of "being in the world, " characterized as "ek-static," in which we function as decentered, non-anthropocentric witnesses to Being. By Heidegger's reckoning, we are mere vehicles or "clearings" in and through which Being intuits its own depths; we are mediums for the disclosure of Being to itself. (Shades of Hegel!) Laing alluded to this late Heideggerian trope in chapter 1 of *The Politics of Experience* when he wrote: "Man creates in transcending himself, in revealing himself. But what he creates, wherefrom and whereto, the clay, the pot and the potter, are all not-me. I am the witness, the medium, the occasion of a happening that the created thing makes evident. Man, most fundamentally, is not engaged in the discovery of what is there, nor in production, nor even in communication, nor in invention. He is enabling being to emerge from nonbeing" (Laing, 1967, p. 42).[3]

Without mentioning Heidegger by name, Laing went on to observe that creative geniuses like Blake, Hölderlin, Rimbaud, Nietzsche, Van Gogh, and Artaud were quite attuned to Being in this ekstatic fashion, but that society, though astonished and thrilled by their efforts, punished them for nonconformity, just as it stigmatizes most forms of "non-egoic" or transcendental experience. The tacit implication of these remarks is that society censures or destroys those creative souls who refuse to extinguish their "inner light." And when Laing later cites the French poet Mallarmé—"L'enfant abdique son ecstase"—one gets the impression that he is using Mallarmé to echo Heidegger once more.

Obviously, there is some truth in these assertions. Given the way the world is presently constituted, to be completely human without subterfuges, defenses, or a "false self" for more than relatively brief interludes is often an extremely risky undertaking, one that invites vulnerability, ostracism, and persecution and incites multiple misunderstandings and misalliances. As Laing noted in *The Divided Self,* even ontologically secure individuals need their "false self" to negotiate the rituals and vicissitudes of daily life.

Nevertheless, Laing's characterization of creative geniuses in *The Politics of Experience* is unfair because it assumes that their madness was purely a function of the fears and the Philistinism of *others*—or to put it more fashionably, perhaps, the Other. Laing did not pause to consider to what extent their personal and existential choices, propensities to self-deception, and so on contributed to their malaise. In short, despite some well-balanced caveats to the contrary, he himself idealized tragic figures who strayed "out of formation."

Moreover, and more to the point, Laing's reverence for creative geniuses poised on the boundaries of *Pleroma* and *Creatura* implies a rather fuzzy and elitist standard for human conduct and experience—one rooted in a visionary sensibility, and therefore one largely irrelevant and unsustainable for the average person. Admittedly, even ordinary folk try to infuse the everyday with pathos and mystery, and to stop the frantic pace of life from time to time to dwell attentively on the mysteries of Being. That is why we meditate, make art, listen to music, and so on. But even if transcendental or "non-egoic" experience was more commonplace in pre-scientific, pre-industrial societies, as Laing and Heidegger maintained, your average Jack and Jill of days gone by were not great artists or religious virtuosi, any more than their modern (or "post-modern") counterparts are. Unless we renounce ordinary work and family commitments, life in any time or place is just too prosaic and too demanding to allow us more than fleeting states of ecstasy. Ecstasy for the masses, à la 1968, makes thrilling rhetoric. But it is not a realistic program, as Laing was well aware. After all, he *divested* himself of political affiliations in 1968, one year after *The Politics of Experience,* never to return to the political arena (Burston, 1996a, ch. 5).

So Laing's debt to Heidegger, like Heidegger himself, is deeply ambiguous. On the one hand, it prompted a healthy skepticism about the prevailing tendency to equate statistical prevalence, or normality, with mental health or genuine sanity. The resulting view suggests that culturally congruent behavior and beliefs are often pseudo-sane adaptations to cultural belief systems that are divorced from existential actualities—adaptations that deprive us of access to deeper, more authentic modes of existence. That contribution, I think, is useful, if only as an antidote to the vapid, one-dimensional thinking about normality that pervades the mental health professions. On the other hand, the Heideggerian thrust of Laing's critique entails an elitist double standard by which merely normal people are invariably found wanting and tormented geniuses are spared the same unforgiving scrutiny reserved for less gifted or eccentric souls. That we safely can do without.

Strangely, despite all the recent controversy, Laing never commented on Heidegger's involvement with the Nazis—at least not to my knowledge. Judging from his interviews with Bob Mullan, Heidegger was closely associated in Laing's mind with Laing's beloved mentor Joe Schorstein, one of Heidegger's close Jewish admirers. Why Schorstein's esteem for Heidegger elevated Heidegger above criticism is not clear. But it certainly seemed to have that effect (Mullan, 1995, ch. 2).

Laing was far less forgiving with Jung, whose involvement with the Nazis he found quite distressing. As he told René Muller in 1979, referring to *The Divided Self* (1960), "I was put off Jung by what I took to be his stance in relationship to Hitler . . . But I've since spent a lot of time studying Jung, and in the forthcoming stuff that I write, I hope to give Jung full credit" (Muller, 1979, p. 13).

Laing never followed through on his intention of giving Jung more credit, because certain discoveries confirmed his worst fears.

While working on a biography of Jung with Eugene Nemeche, Laing stumbled across some previously suppressed documents that amply attested to the depth and sincerity of Jung's Nazi ties in the early 1930s. In view of recent disclosures, it seems likely that these documents are all in the public domain now, and that Jung has no more skeletons concealed in this particular closet.[4] But as Ralph Metzner recalls, Laing was so incensed about his discoveries that he publicly abused John Weir Perry, a well-known Jungian, whose work on metanoia preceded his own (Metzner in Mullan, 1997).

Arguably, Laing's attitude toward Heidegger differed from his attitude toward Jung because he did *not* consider Jung a theorist of the same order or ability as Freud, Sartre, or Heidegger. As he said to Richard Evans in 1976, he found Jung's minimization of the personal unconscious and dismissal of Freudian dream theory too cavalier. And he avoided using Jung's introvert/extrovert typology because he found it "brilliant and dangerous"—provocative and fertile, yet seductively *overexplanatory* (Evans, 1976, pp. 11–12). To Bob Mullan, in 1988, Laing complained that Jung's writing was leaden and disappointing, stylistically speaking, and that Jung's attitude toward Nietzsche was deeply patronizing (Mullan, 1995, p. 104).

Nevertheless, and by his own admission, Laing took very seriously Jung's theory of archetypes and the collective unconscious, and said that anyone who approaches the operations and contents of the human mind phenomenologically is bound to discover them eventually (Evans, 1976, pt. 1). At the same time, he thought that the whole field was still "up for grabs" and hoped that someone suitably talented and insightful would eventually sort it out. The odd thing about these sentiments is how they reflect on Laing's relationship to Sartre. Sartre's *Critique of Dialectical Reason,* which Laing and Cooper first summarized for English readers, proscribes on methodological grounds the invocation of any collective or supra-individual subject. It categorically rules out Jung's "collective unconscious" as a seductive metaphor, at best, and a deliberate mystification at worst.

On the face of it, then, Laing affirmed the validity of both Jung and Sartre without considering the contradictions that would inevitably ensue. This underscores the point I made in *The Wing of Madness,* that contrary to appearances, Laing's theories of schizophrenia are not all of a piece. Formerly, however, I stressed that there is an insurmountable tension between the (mostly earlier) existential and (mostly later) social constructivist models. I still hold that view. Now, on a somewhat different note, I am stressing the fact that there is a basic contradiction between what I previously termed the neo-Jungian and phenomenological approaches, which were advanced more or less simultaneously (Burston, 1996a, ch. 11).

Once again, I hasten to add that the tensions and contradictions between these various models of madness do not automatically invalidate them all. On the contrary: it obliges us to sift through them carefully and consider each on its own merits. But in order to do this properly, we must remember that *Sanity, Madness and the Family* was based on a methodology that Laing and Esterson termed "social phenomenology," which is principally indebted to Husserl and Sartre and therefore refrains from positing the existence of any supra-individual "group mind," or from making interpretations about meanings, motives, or desires of which the individuals who are being studied are unconscious (Laing and Esterson, 1964, introduction). And while it stressed the social intelligibility of patients' symptoms and gave them a breathtaking coherence seldom found in analytic case histories, it by no means necessitated the view that a patient's madness—real or alleged—is an abortive attempt at self-cure.

By contrast, the neo-Jungian or metanoia theory construed madness as an inner journey, or one occurring in "inner space," rather than as a social artifact occurring in the social domain. In his own words: "This journey is experienced as going further 'in,' as going back through one's personal life, in and back and through and beyond into the experience of all mankind, of the primal man, of Adam and perhaps even further into the realms of animals, vegetables and minerals" (Laing, 1967, p. 126).

Careful consideration of the metanoia model does not necessarily elicit or compel any interest in a symptom's social intelligibility. If a person has been thrust out of normal social space into a timeless, archetypal realm, and is consumed in his mental commerce with phylogenetic imagos, there is no need (and no warrant) to suppose that his bizarre ideation is an alienated apperception of the ensemble of social relations that obtained in his personal past. In fact, to the contrary, there are very good reasons *not* to make this assumption.

Despite their disparate emphases, the phenomenological and neo-Jungian models, which appeared in simultaneous but separate publications (Laing, 1964; Laing and Esterson, 1964), were deliberately interwoven in chapter 5 of *The Politics of Experience* (1967). Plainly, Laing saw no contradiction between them—at this stage, anyway. And strange to say, though he did not invent it, Laing probably rose to fame on the strength of the metanoia model, whose appeal resides in the fact that it resonates with accounts of prototypical inner journeys (culminating in shattering and/or exquisite epiphanies) found in Eastern and Western mysticism, Romantic poetry and literature, and last but not least, the diverse publications of the psychedelic era, which drew and embellished on these earlier sources, often in a regrettably lurid fashion.

Does that mean that this model is irrelevant, scientifically speaking? No. But in retrospect, it is obvious that it allows therapist and patient alike much more latitude for speculation, imagination, and sheer invention than does the ascetic rigor of the social-phenomenological approach. It is also interesting to note that in his final publication, a brief but illuminating summary of his life's work entitled "Laing's Understanding of Interpersonal Experience" (1987), Laing stressed the centrality of social phenomenology and left metanoia completely out of his account. I doubt that this was a deliberate omission. But it is a pretty accurate reflection of what is genuinely Laingian in Laing's writings.

Finally, no discussion of Laing and modern Gnosticism would be complete without some mention of Jacques Lacan (Lacan, 1978; Schneiderman, 1984). I am not suggesting that Lacan *influenced* Laing. But here and there the resemblances are striking, and attributable to the fact that Lacan was also influenced by Heidegger and Sartre, albeit in different ways (Borch-Jacobsen, 1991). The Gnostic element in Lacan is his characterization of the ego as an "imaginary function," a creature of "specular identification," or an illusory and artificial construct embedded in "the discourse of the other." Lacan said the goal of analysis was to deconstruct the ego, rather than to support and strengthen it, as Freud and his followers had enjoined. This therapeutic objective echoes the ancient Gnostic view that all but a handful of *cogniscenti* fundamentally misrecognize themselves and their condition. They imagine that they are free, that they know who they are, but their sense of identity is a chimera born of unconscious subjection.

Laing's hostility to ego psychology bears an obvious resemblance to Lacan's. But to his credit, I think, Laing did not attribute his antinomian ideas on this score to Freud, then stake his identity and reputation on a muddled and exaggerated notion of fidelity to him.[5] Moreover, despite his earlier overtures to Lacan, Laing, like Sartre, saw the ego as a largely illusory entity, but did not dismiss the existence of the self (Sartre, 1936). How could he? Sartrean existentialism would be utterly vacuous without the concepts of consciousness and human agency, and so would Laingian thought.

As a matter of historical interest, note that Sartre's distinction between the ego and the self emerged from his critique of Husserl. As noted previously, Husserl maintained that the ego can consciously "bracket" all of its contents and operations save the act of bracketing itself. Sartre, by contrast, argued that a consistent application of Husserlian method discloses that the ego is an artifact of consciousness, not its *source* (Sartre, 1936). While he may have been following Husserl's lead, Sartre's conclusion was strikingly Nietzschean. By Sartre's reckoning the ego is a fiction, a story we tell ourselves for defensive purposes. At the risk of oversimplifying Sartre's discussion, the entity that concocts the story that the ego consists in is the real self.

Not to be outdone, Lacan radicalized Sartre's critique of Husserl by eliminating the self as well. The problem with this position is that if you eliminate the self completely you cannot explain human consciousness or human agency effectively, except as an epiphenomenon of nonpersonal processes or entities-in-relation (which is what structuralism attempted to do).[6] In recent years, poststructuralist thinkers have also gained prominence proclaiming "the death of Man" or "the death of the subject." Unfortunately, those who pursue psychology in this spirit are destined to lapse into equivocation, incoherence, or evasion of various kinds, which are rendered plausible by spuriously assigning qualities to analogous processes that have been banished by fiat to parts of *impersonal systems* rather than actual persons. Or they may simply refuse to deal with them by declaring consciousness and agency to be illusions.

While we cannot discount on purely logical grounds the possibility that selfhood, consciousness, and agency are illusions, it is strange to hear representatives of these schools declare these ideas to be "repressive." To characterize something as an illusion is one thing, but to call it "repressive" implies the existence of a coercive relation between two (or more) persons in which one attempts to modify the beliefs and practices of the other(s). Alternatively, in Freudian terms, it implies a single person who seeks to annul or deny the experience of certain intimate or deeply felt desires, intentions, beliefs, and so on in deference to inner fears and/or ideals relating to other persons who have been "internalized" in the process of socialization.

In other words, even the Freudian idea of repression, which verges on a monadology in its metapsychological form, cannot completely erase the interpersonal nexus within which "repression" takes place. But if persons are not actually present here, as our critics claim, and if the interpersonal nexus within which our experience and intentions are articulated are nothing but a series of circuits in a vast social machinery, then no one is being repressed, and conversely, no one is repressing anyone—themselves included. Since the objection is vacuous, semantically speaking, what could account for the vehemence that often accompanies such accusations?

In addition to implying the existence of persons-in-relation, the idea of "repression" implies a latent value system, one predicated on the idea that freedom from illusions is a vital precondition for emancipation. The question then becomes: emancipation from what? And for whom? If persons do not exist, finally, what possible rationale can there be for critique, for struggle, for emancipation or liberation in any form?

As recent scholarship indicates, much of the impetus for post-structuralist and postmodern thought stems from the French appropriation of the later Heidegger (Soper, 1986; Rockmore, 1995). The claims made by these thinkers far exceed those of Marx, Freud, and their followers, who claimed that consciousness and agency are permeated and/or vitiated by illusions—a claim that experience and good sense unfortunately confirm all too often. By contrast, the newer breed takes no prisoners and leaves nothing standing in its totalizing zeal. By these thinker's reckoning, consciousness and agency are themselves the illusions that need to be dispelled or "deconstructed." Despite his indebtedness to Heidegger, and his deep admiration for Michel Foucault, Laing shied away from this conclusion and retained consciousness and agency as proverbial bedrock, rather than mere epiphenomena.

Why? First, note that by a curious coincidence, Sartre's distinction between the ego and the self converges with the psychoanalytic formulations of Jung and Winnicott. Like Sartre, though for different reasons, Jung and Winnicott both distinguished between the ego and the self, and Laing found their formulations quite useful clinically. So by Laing's reckoning, the fact that the conscious ego is largely an illusory entity born of unconscious fear and vanity, and fashioned in the struggle for survival, does not nullify the existence of the self, though it does obstruct access to it much of the time.

Another factor involved in Laing's reluctance to join forces with his French contemporaries was his indebtedness to Martin Buber and John MacMurray, which operated on two levels. Laing was aware that the argument that selfhood, consciousness, and agency are not primary data but artifactual and illusory is defensible on purely logical grounds. And to the best of my knowledge, he never questioned the validity of such an approach in sociology, anthropology, economics, and so on. But if *The Divided Self,* The *Politics of Experience,* and *The Voice of Experience* are any indication, Laing did not see how a psychology worthy of the name could be developed on these unlikely foundations. To paraphrase Laing himself, our experience *is* our psyche. The experience of consciousness and of personal agency is a self-validating, self-authenticating certainty that requires no support or sanction from the natural sciences. To invalidate our experience by trying to reduce or annul these elementary features of consciousness in deference to natural science does violence to our selves and to others, and is not genuinely scientific.

Laing made these points with great eloquence and conviction, to be sure. But Buber and MacMurray said similar things in the forties and fifties, and their insight and example spurred him on. Upon reflection, it becomes apparent that Laing's rejoinders to natural scientism in psychology could apply equally to structuralism, poststructuralism, postmodernism, and deconstructionism, which attempt to annul the experience of consciousness, agency, selfhood, and so on by treating them as the epiphenomena of *social* structures and systems, rather than as purely natural ones. So while Laing felt a greater degree of kinship with these more recent trends, he refrained from joining them wholeheartedly lest he undermine the very basis of his own critical project.

Another feature of Laing's indebtedness to Buber and Mac-

Murray bears closely on Laing's religious sensibilities. Buber and MacMurray's views were predicated on very similar forms of theistic personalism: Buber's foundation was Jewish, and MacMurray's was Christian. Despite his varied reputation as a militant atheist or an eclectic mystic, Laing actually spent much of his life as a reluctant and often anguished agnostic who longed for the consolations of faith and a personal relation to God. The concepts of selfhood and salvation are correlative, however, and the whole ethical structure of the Judeo-Christian inheritance is meaningless without the concept of free human agency. To reject the concept of selfhood as conceived by Buber and MacMurray would have been a symbolic foreclosure on this avenue of possible transcendence, and this he could (or would) not do.

Reviewing these influences and affinities in sequence, it is safe to conclude that Laing's Gnostic leanings rendered him more persuasive when he described what genuine sanity is *not* than when he was making positive pronouncements about it. His chief contribution to the notion of sanity probably lay in refusing to treat mental health and normality as synonyms, and in suspending or inverting our commonsense assumptions about normality to see where these transgressive thoughts would lead. In the process, Laing insisted that statistical averageness or cultural congruence often harbors hidden losses by creating an equivocal pseudo-sanity wrought from complicity in "social phantasy systems." He wasn't the only one who viewed normality in this skeptical fashion. At the time he was writing, this perception was widespread and integral to the zeitgeist. Many contemporaries—for example, Erich Fromm, Herbert Marcuse, Paul Goodman, C. Wright Mills, and Jules Henry—took a very dim view of normality in the Cold War era.

Nowadays, unfortunately, many feel that the skeptical attitude toward normality Laing advocated was *merely* a zeitgeist phenomenon, and therefore no longer relevant. But Laing thought of his views not as the expression of a "sixties" sensibility, or of a trendy, adolescent radicalism, but as an expression of "the perennial philosophy." In an interview with Douglas Kirsner, he remarked: "If we take the world's well-known spiritual teachers from the Buddha to the Judaeo-Christian tradition, to the Greek tradition and the Islamic tradition, it is said all over the place that most people by any rigorous standard are pretty daft . . . so I don't think I am saying anything unusual here" (Laing in Mullan, 1997, p. 43).

Granted, it was not new. And in all spiritual traditions, celebrated saints and sages claim that most of us are deeply, often willfully estranged from reality; that we live in spiritual darkness and
obscurity while imagining that we inhabit the clear light of day.
Moreover, these luminaries all liken the condition of the normal
man (or woman) to a state of unwitting imprisonment or servitude,
stressing that our self-estrangement is caused by our tendencies to
make a fetish of the ego and to deepen our ignorance (of ourselves
and the world) by indulging our propensities to vanity, fear, and
greed.

But stressing similarities, as Laing did, obscures important differences both between and within traditions. Take the Judeo-
Christian tradition. As I noted in *The Wing of Madness,* the Jewish
and Christian faiths (and their respective denominations) are
fraught with the tension between Messianic and Gnostic sensibilities. The Messianic outlook is rooted in the prophetic temper. It
maintains that all people are made in God's image, it is passion-
ately concerned with social justice, and it is actually or incipiently
democratic in character, expecting God's will to be implemented in
historical time in ways that disclose the truth and that will rally *all*
of humanity to its senses. When social conditions render the realization of the Messianic hope impractical, this leveling tendency
takes on an otherworldly expression: the idea that all of us are
equal in the eyes of God, and that no one, however proud or privi-
leged, is intrinsically worthier than anyone else—or that if such differences do exist, they are determined by our actions and ethical
bearing, rather than the things of this world, and will be noted impartially on the Day of Judgment.

Though somewhat tangential to our discussion, note that the
Messianic insistence that we are all made in God's image and therefore of equal worth fostered the modern political demand for equal
rights. But the ideas of equal worth and/or equal rights ought not
to be confused with the bizarre notion that we are somehow all the
same. Equality and sameness are not equivalent terms or concepts,
and as Buber's notion of dialogue makes plain, sameness has no
place in the Messianic perspective (Avnon, 1998). Like all animal
species, we are demonstrably different in size, shape, weight, color,
and more importantly, in traits like intelligence, curiosity, sociability, courage, compliance, and loyalty. To ignore these differences is
sheer folly. Nevertheless, the fact that we are all of essentially equal

worth and endowed—ideally—with equal rights, necessitates the corollary assumption that we are all equally responsible for ourselves, and for what we make of what we are made of.

By contrast with the Messianic weltanschauung, the Gnostic outlook is closer to the spirit of Greek religion and philosophy, and to Orphism and Platonism in particular. It views the temporal sphere as inherently and irremediably corrupt, and governed by the will to power—St. Augustine's *libido dominandi*. Accordingly, while it distrusts worldly authority, it regards movements for social justice and transformation as either futile or contrary to nature. In lieu of earthly hopes and aspirations, the Gnostic outlook cultivates a "disincarnate" spirituality, one predicated on a radical distrust of the flesh and its appetites. And instead of a democratic (or incipiently democratic) ethos, it promotes a hierarchical conception of humanity, insisting that there are grades or levels of consciousness (like those Plato proposed in the *Republic.*) This elitist ethos is eternally wary and vigilant against leveling tendencies and the incursions of democratic movements and institutions. In the Gnostic's mind, the spiritual adept does not live on the same plane, or follow the same rules, as "normal" people, who are hopelessly inured to their spiritual subjection.

Admittedly, these characterizations of the Messianic and Gnostic sensibilities are highly schematic. They are ideal types, and as such are often applied to thinkers who evince most (but not all) of the above-mentioned traits, including the characteristic anti-Semitism of the ancient Gnostics (Jonas, 1974, ch. 13). Like all binary classifications—such as Jung's introvert-extrovert typology—this one can be overexplanatory and blind us to concurrent cultural and social processes that shape prevailing patterns of thought. Even so, it is quite illuminating when applied to the history and psychology of religion, to contemporary concepts of the numinous, and last, but not least, to twentieth-century thought and letters.

To a very large extent, the history of Judaism and Christianity reflects the conflict and compromise between these two spiritual orientations, which have struggled and combined in various ways. Sometimes one or another predominates vividly, but mostly they coexist with the lines between them exceedingly blurred, because organized religion must minimize or ignore the disparities between them to maintain a semblance of cosmological coherence—or even deny their coexistence in the same body of believers. As a result, we have to study the history of heretical sects and mystical movements that diverge from the mainstream before these orientations come clearly into view once more (see, for example, Bloch, 1972; Cohn, 1970).

Another factor that obscures the relevance of this typology is the process of secularization. Because of secularization, most of us have never committed ourselves to or even resonated with either of these religious sensibilities, singly or sequentially. Most who are aware of their existence regard them as relics of the past, rather than as powerful cultural templates that, in subdued or sublimated form, feed the subterranean currents of our intellectual life even in our current "postmodern" constellation.

If pressed, however, a man like Laing would undoubtedly have recognized these conflicting currents within himself. The Messianic sensibility is deeply embedded in the more worldly and democratic forms of Calvinism that still flourish in his native Scotland, and in the Hasidic spirituality that Laing learned from Joseph Schorstein, his mentor in philosophy and neurosurgery. And on reflection, one simply cannot find more vivid examples of the conflict and compromise between the Messianic and the Gnostic outlooks than in the different varieties of Hasidism and Calvinism.[7]

Because the religious sensibilities that shaped and informed Laing's work are seldom discussed overtly in his books, one has to look elsewhere to discern them. As a ferocious satire, Clancy Sigal's fictional account of his ultimately abortive therapy and collaboration with Laing in the Kingsley Hall era, *Zone of the Interior,* is unreliable on the level of quotidian facts. But if you make allowance for the elements of farce and caricature, it does convey the weird fusion of brashly hopeful evangelical fervor and the arrogant, even cynical otherworldly elitism that animated Laing and his followers throughout the sixties. Admittedly, Laing's religious imagery was often injudiciously mixed with revolutionary rhetoric, a tendency that was less conspicuous after 1968—not just in Laing, but in the culture as a whole. Yet even in the seventies and eighties, the dedicated Laing watcher gets glimpses of these religious sensibilities, shorn of their earlier political (or pseudo-political) overtones, in numerous interviews he gave and in the occasional talk or book review.

But even if Laing were not raised as a Presbyterian, and had not assimilated Hasidism vicariously through Schorstein, he would have encountered the Messianic and Gnostic mentalities in the work of Martin Buber and Martin Heidegger. Buber's Messianic roots require no discussion, but Heidegger's Gnostic affinities still may, because of the objections that loyal Heideggerians may have to Hans Jonas's insightful commentary. They will note, for example, that Heidegger commended Nietzsche for discrediting once and for all Platonic otherworldliness and dualistic metaphysics and insist that this invalidates the Gnostic label, Jonas notwithstanding.

If this bit of evidence stood alone, it would indeed signal a fundamental divergence of outlook. But other circumstances cast doubt on this verdict. For example, in *Being and Time,* Heidegger frequently castigates *das Mann* for its "worldliness," implying that authentic existence is otherworldly in character. Admittedly, Heidegger does not actually say so in so many words. But his repeated use of the adjective "worldly" indicates that he finds "worldliness" a contemptible trait. In short, Heidegger condemns *das Mann* for worldliness and commends Nietzsche for abjuring otherworldliness. And the deeper we probe on religious questions, the more labyrinthian ambiguities we encounter, rendering it impossible to classify Heidegger as either a worldly or otherworldly thinker.

Does *that* settle the issue then? Decidedly not. Otherworldliness is only one of various traits or tropes characteristic of the Gnostic mentality. On other points, the resemblance is very close indeed. And clearly, Heidegger was not alone in his Gnostic tendencies. In different ways, and for different reasons, Nietzsche, Heidegger, and Jung all rejected the Messianic dimension in Western culture and embraced a predominantly Gnostic orientation. In developing sedulously along these lines, they enriched twentieth-century thought immeasurably, and Laing drew extensively on them for inspiration and insight. This was entirely to Laing's credit. One cannot fault him for putting them to good use.

Unfortunately, despite its undoubted intellectual power, the Gnostic mentality is also an equivocal and potentially dangerous one, and Laing did not seem to notice any of the negative consequences of Nietzsche's, Heidegger's, and Jung's rejection of the Messianic. An obvious consequence historically is the drift toward fascism. If we set aside all the lame excuses, all the special pleading that is so common nowadays, there is something about modern

Gnosticism (or its more recent manifestations) that lends solace, inspiration, and credence to Nazism and its kindred movements and manifestations. And though the Gnostic sensibility sharpened Laing's critique of normality, it muddled his concept—or rather, concepts—of mental health.

R. D. LAING AND THE CRISIS
OF PSYCHOTHERAPY

··· 6 ···

Despite many years of research and reflection, the fact remains that there is still no single unambiguous definition of "normality" that enables us to assess impartially whether a particular pattern of behavior is really normal or not. Instead, as we saw previously, there are several such definitions, which are all compressed or conflated into the same multivalent word—definitions whose divergent and overlapping significations change profoundly depending on the context and the speaker. This strange state of affairs need not deter clinicians from going about their business. Their services are needed urgently, and they must do the best they can with the tools they have. Still, in defining something or someone as "abnormal," everything depends on what we mean by the term normal (Canguilhem, 1966).

A similar situation obtains with the concept of mental health. As we saw in the previous chapter, the terms "normality" and "mental health" are not necessarily synonymous, though many clinicians and researchers assume that they are. As a result, the "mental health" professions are incorrigibly vague and reticent when attempting to define what mental health actually is, but are remarkably prolific in their efforts to describe and enumerate the varieties of mental illness. Just survey the American scene over the last half-century. The first edition of the *Diagnostic and Statistical Manual of Mental Disorders,* or *DSM,* published by the American Psychiatric Association in 1952, contained 106 categories of mental disorder. The second edition, published in 1968, had 182. The third edition, published in 1980, had 265. The revised third edition—really a fourth edition—published in 1987, had 292, while the (so-called) fourth edition, published in 1993, has 347. That is an increase of 241 categories—more than triple the initial number—in less than fifty years, with an average of about 48 new categories of mental disorder in each new edition.

This hectic pace cannot be sustained indefinitely. But even at half the present rate—say 24 new categories per edition, and a new edition every decade or so—just imagine how many mental disorders will be listed by the end of the twenty-first century. Many mental health professionals see the most recent edition of the *DSM*—really the fifth, though it is called the fourth—as the crowning glory of their collective labors. Still, one wonders what would happen if they devoted more of their energy and resources to understanding mental health.[1]

Meanwhile, some critics say that the *DSM* is intolerably bloated and ambiguous, and argue that a genuine taxonomy of mental disorder, one more cogent and concise, can be developed through factor analysis, provided we scrap the *DSM* and start fresh. If true, this would be an enormous improvement on the present state of affairs. After all, the fact that we have more and more categories of mental disorder does not necessarily mean that we understand it better. In many instances, no doubt, it merely provides a more impressive camouflage for our ignorance, or more sophisticated pretexts for conducting business as usual.

But even a taxonomy crafted in conformity with Ockham's rule —"We should not needlessly multiply (hypothetical) entities"— must eventually reckon with the essential circularity of our definitions of normality and abnormality. Furthermore, those who develop it must eventually decide whether, or to what extent and under what circumstances, normality and mental health actually overlap or coincide.

Does Laing have anything to offer us on these questions? He seldom addressed them directly, and never gave them the sustained attention they deserve. But read carefully, and in sequence, his works provide an oblique but illuminating commentary on the issues that *need* to be raised in order to make some headway on them. As it happens, a close reading of these texts discloses not one but two models of mental health. The first model, in *The Divided*

Self, is the most explicit and readily intelligible. But by the time of *The Politics of Experience,* it has been abandoned in favor of another, slightly less explicit one that takes some exegetical effort to bring it to light.

Let us start at the beginning. In *The Divided Self,* Laing assumed that mental health coincides with what he calls "primary ontological security." According to Laing, ontologically secure people have a firm and stable sense of identity, a secure feeling of personal autonomy, and a capacity for genuine self-disclosure. They are not terrified of intimacy or beset by nagging anxiety and doubt as to who (or what) they are. In addition, they are able to sustain good-enough interpersonal relationships and can seek pleasure and gratification within the framework of these relationships. While they may reify (and be reified by) others and develop a false-self—or selves—to adapt to situations in which authenticity is proscribed, they do not feel fatally compromised as a result. They wear their masks comfortably, using them as vehicles for achieving their own ends and shedding them whenever circumstances permit. As a result, there is a good deal of confluence between their "being-for-themselves" and their "being-for-others" in most social contexts, and they alternate comfortably between solitude and sociability.

By contrast, ontologically insecure or "schizoid" people have a shaky sense of identity. They fear intimacy and self-disclosure, lest they be engulfed, petrified, or otherwise impinged upon by others and their precarious sense of autonomy irrevocably shattered. Accordingly, they route more and more of their emotional and intellectual commerce with others through their false selves, using a semblance of sociability as a camouflage whose purpose is to ensure the "real" self's survival. The schizoid person imagines that his "real" self—his "being-for-himself"—can be only be experienced and expressed in solitude, utterly disengaged from his publicly observable self. In fact, notes Laing, the more "free" and detached this "real" self becomes, the more enveloped it is in a phantasy world, and the less capable it is of commitment or risk in the interpersonal domain. Moreover, since the communal self is also perforce corporeal, the schizoid person must conceive of his "real" self as essentially *disembodied.* This process can be sustained within a relatively sane adaptation to the world, provided the patient can still distinguish fact from phantasy. But as the chasm deepens between the private and public selves, between one's being-for-oneself and one's being-for-others, the schizoid person becomes progressively estranged from consensually validated reality and may lapse into frank psychosis.

When Laing wrote *The Divided Self* in the late 1950s, there were a few epidemiological studies attesting to the prevalence of mental disorder in the general population. But since to my knowledge he never referred to them, we can assume that he was either unaware of these studies or simply not inclined to take them seriously. In any event, at this stage, like the majority of his peers, Laing thought of mental health and normality as synonyms. Accordingly, he referred to ontological security as the "normal" state of affairs and argued that the ability to identify with one's body, to sustain good-enough interpersonal relationships, to alternate between solitude and sociability, and to seek and to enjoy some congruence between one's being-for-oneself and being-for-others are constitutive of mental health and preferable to the schizoid or schizophrenic experience.

But in *Self and Others,* published in 1961, Laing ceased to define normality as a state of ontological security and began to describe it as the state of occupying a "tenable position" in a social phantasy system. Normal people, though less tormented than their disturbed counterparts, are so deeply embedded in social phantasy systems that their sense of autonomy, identity, and personal agency are largely illusory. This argument was repeated with even greater emphasis in *The Politics of Experience* (1967), which stressed how equivocal and impoverished is the sanity of the average person. For Laing, the "normal" person in contemporary society enjoys a state of "pseudo-sanity" that fosters the atrophy of critical thinking, precludes the possibility of genuine transcendence, and promotes violence through the demonization of those who do not belong to one's own reference group. Accordingly, he now said that true sanity is not predicated on the ability to shed one's false self intermittently, as circumstances allow, but radically and completely, until the false self or ego "dies" or is transcended in a spiritual *katabasis* that takes one "inward" and "downward," rather than "up" and "outward." (Note again the resemblance to Jung). One can pursue this goal deliberately, through spiritual disciplines, or be thrust involuntarily on this descent into an "inner space" in a process that, if properly facilitated, results in a rebirth and reintegration of the personality. Laing's once famous epigram from *The Bird of Paradise*—"If I could turn you on, if I could drive you out of your wretched mind, if I could tell you, I would let you know"—was partly intended to express the idea that absent the requisite inner journey and the resulting self-transformation, true sanity will elude us forever.

Though Laing did not openly acknowledge the shift, it is apparent that the notion of mental health he was working with in 1967 was very different from its precursor. True sanity, by this later reckoning, is exceptional rather than statistically average. It no longer requires identification with one's body, but it does require the ability to transcend the ego (or false self) before the search for equilibrium restores one's capacity for sociability, good-enough interpersonal relationships, and so on.

Let us survey the strengths and weaknesses of both models of sanity. Laing's first model provided us with the following criteria of mental health:

1. identification with one's body,
2. a stable sense of autonomy, identity, and personal agency,
3. a capacity for genuine self-disclosure,
4. a capacity for sustaining good-enough intimate relationships, and
5. significant congruence or overlap between one's being-for-oneself and one's being-for-others.

These are excellent criteria and not to be lightly discarded. Laing himself never rejected them explicitly, even though he apparently felt that he outgrew them. Nevertheless, despite Laing's vigorous objections to taxonomies of mental disorder, *The Divided Self* inadvertently provided readers with a binary system of classification—ontologically secure versus insecure—that like all binary systems, is overexplanatory if taken in isolation. This classification conflated statistical normality with a state of mental health, despite a complete lack of evidence for this commonsense assumption. Perhaps sometime in 1960 it dawned on Laing that the tendency to confound or conflate "normality" and "mental health" is a product of what Husserl termed the "natural attitude" that has been smuggled surreptitiously into the "theoretical attitude" or scientific weltanschauung. And perhaps this realization contributed to his hasty (and unfortunate) abandonment of his earlier work on ontological insecurity, which was so full of promise.

In contrast to its predecessor, Laing's second model of mental health *inverted* commonsense assumptions and assumed that mental health, far from being normal, is actually quite rare. Writing in the midst of the Vietnam War and the U.S.-Soviet arms race, Laing insisted that a statistically average person can sustain the semblance of "good enough" interpersonal relations with like-minded people while being (1) profoundly estranged from his or her own experience, (2) incapable of thinking critically about his or her own cultural and social surroundings, and (3) actively paranoid, hateful, and genocidal toward members of out-groups.

The problem is that Laing did not think through the implications of this shift or try to integrate his new perception of normality and his old definition of mental health. Instead it appears that he simply jettisoned ontological security and construed sanity as something that occurs largely outside of and/or against the prevailing order, rather than as a state of being that flourishes comfortably within it. Granted, there are times when prevailing ideologies are so radically at variance with the truth that it is hard not to credit this approach with some validity. But this new position makes mental health an inherently exceptional achievement that is attainable only by a small minority. It is therefore quite elitist in tone. To put it crudely, if losing your mind is a prerequisite to saving your soul, most of us cannot be bothered. For the average adult, the dedicated practice of spiritual discipline is too time-consuming or irrelevant at the moment, and the prospect of being mad is too aversive to be taken seriously.

Another, closely related problem was that the subtle but profound shift in Laing's views on sanity entailed some major modifications in his ideas about psychotherapy. As a result, there are three relatively distinct treatment approaches embedded in his work, in which the goals of treatment are

1. sanity as the restoration of relatedness, the recovery of authentic conscience, and so forth *(The Divided Self)*,
2. sanity as the end product of a metanoic journey *(The Politics of Experience)*, and
3. the evocation of birth and intrauterine traumas *(The Facts of Life* and *The Voice of Experience.)*

These therapeutic frameworks are probably of very unequal value. The first is in many respects the most promising, and despite his debts to earlier thinkers, the most original—though Laing might not have thought so given the dramatic shift in his views and his compulsion to outdo himself with each new book. As we have seen, the second model, though more derivative in the way it leans on Jung, can be tamed and pruned so that it becomes defensible and usefully provocative. The third, by contrast, is "iffy," as Laing would say. Though it is full of intriguing conjectures, it completely evades rather than confronts the considerable tension between the preceding two approaches and periods of his work. Regrettably, little of enduring value can be salvaged for posterity unless we grapple with the tensions between the first two models.

At first glance, Laing's about-face in abandoning ontological security as the defining attribute of sanity seems to preclude any compromise or negotiation between his first and second positions. And perhaps it does. But in fairness to Laing, the fact that they are *logically* antagonistic does not preclude their peaceful coexistence under the umbrella of a pluralistic pragmatism that underscored much of Laing's clinical practice. In a nutshell, this attitude suggests that patients whose sense of self is still relatively strong should be helped to recover within and retain that framework for existence and to enjoy their lives to the utmost. Really tormented or creative people, for whom simple pleasures are elusive or ephemeral, may need a different framework to work within before they can again tackle the issues of interpersonal relatedness.

Though this approach hardly resolves the glaring contradictions that confront us here, one can see how Laing arrived at this expedient accommodation. Laing's notion of ontological security was a persuasive effort to give content and specificity to commonsense notions of sanity, and to put them on a solid philosophical footing. Most patients need this. It strikes them as plausible and reassuring, and gives them hope of achieving some of their most cherished goals. By contrast, sanity as the end-product of a metanoic process discredits the commonsense equation of sanity and normality, and this makes many patients—and most professionals—profoundly uncomfortable, though it may be indispensable when working with psychotics. Laing may have lacked the consistency or motivation to reconcile these positions, but if we bring a little imagination to bear, perhaps we can integrate the best features of both models by blending some elements and discarding others. For the sake of argument, then, let us suppose true sanity entails

1. a stable sense of autonomy, identity, and personal agency,
2. capacity for self-disclosure,
3. capacity for sustaining good-enough personal relationships,
4. significant congruence or overlap between one's being-for-oneself and one's being-for-others,
5. a refusal and/or inability to polarize humanity and demonize out-groups, and
6. an ability to think critically about one's own society, to "see through" social phantasy systems, and to tolerate the social and emotional consequences.

Finally, let us stipulate that in contrast to statistical normality or conflict-free adaptation, true sanity is relatively rare but does *not* require a prolonged metanoic voyage to achieve—though it does not preclude one either. (Identification with one's body might also be an optional feature, depending on the person's religious background, among other things.)

It should still be apparent that true sanity does not immunize anyone from suffering or internal conflict. On the contrary, a vivid awareness of life's complexities, of the prevalence of evil and injustice, and of the tragedy, fragility, sheer waste, and absurdity of so much of human existence creates possibilities for anguish unimagined by "well-adjusted" individuals. It also heightens the sense of the comic and the absurd. So perhaps our emerging (though still elusive) sense of sanity is destined to be dialectical: it will embrace opposing yet deeply intertwined polarities including optimism, a sense of humor, and a negative capability.

Before speculating further along these lines, however, we would be wise to contextualize the search for sanity in Laing's discussion of existential needs (Burston, 1996a, ch. 9). The term "existential needs" was coined by Erich Fromm to denote generic human needs, which hinge on our awareness of death and our need to transcend our mere facticity—our given, "creaturely" status—by becoming "creators" in our own right (Burston, 1991, ch. 4). Existential needs are not reducible to the exigencies of mere drive satisfaction and are not phase or stage specific: instead, they are enduring and intrinsic to human nature in all times and places. Indeed, Fromm said that the nonsatisfaction of existential needs gradually erodes our sanity and deepens our tendencies toward destructiveness and depersonalization.

Laing discussed six such "existential needs" at length, including, (1) a need for authentic self-disclosure and (2) a need for the confirmation of one's power to give, or "make a difference" to another. These two needs logically presuppose a third—namely, (3) a need for relatedness to others—since self-disclosure and the experience of "potency" in this specifically interpersonal sense cannot occur in a vacuum. According to this reading, in which Fromm and Laing concur, our sociability is not merely the secondary consequence of our organismic attempts to satisfy tissue needs for food, warmth, sex, and so on, as it was for Freud, but a psychological motive sui generis (Burston, 1991, ch. 4).

In addition to these needs, Laing also discussed (4) a need for ontological security, and a corollary sense of agency, autonomy, and self-worth, (5) need for transcendence, and (6) a need for truth and freedom from deception. The need for truth (and the adverse consequences of being subject to sustained deception) is a constant theme in Laing's work, and while scarcely irrelevant here, it is not particularly problematic. The other two are, however. From the standpoint of those who are ontologically secure, transcendental or "non-egoic" experience is optional or superfluous. Many who enjoy a robust sense of selfhood do very well without it, thank you very much. And conversely, from the transcendental standpoint, the need for ontological security is also deeply suspect. If the sense of agency, autonomy, and identity it confers are mere illusions that enable spiritual invalids to hobble through life, then the status of ontological security as an "existential need" becomes moot at best.

And so, on reflection, we discover that the existential needs that Laing emphasized at different periods of his career become optional or superfluous, depending on which model of sanity we adopt. That being so, we will bracket the controversial ones as "optional," while retaining the other four as "basic." Provisionally then, human beings are animated by four existential needs, over and above the imperatives of mere bodily survival: (1) a need for relatedness to others, (2) a need for authentic self-disclosure, (3) a need for interpersonal efficacy, a sense of potency, or being able to "make a difference" to others, and (4) a need for truth (or freedom from deception). On the face of it, perhaps, the need for ontological security is more compatible with this list than the need for transcendence (or non-egoic) experience. After all, transcendental experience does not necessarily confer a greater desire or ability for relatedness, self-disclosure, and so on, though if it is genuine, it may deepen our ability or desire to discern the truth and not get caught up in conventional lies and appearances.

Then why all the fuss about transcendence of the ego? Too much LSD, perhaps? Admittedly, many of Laing's reflections on transcendental or (non-egoic) experience were published during the psychedelic era. But Laing was interested in non-egoic experience long before he experimented with drugs, and he spent a year of his life in the serious and single-minded study of meditation. More to the point here, the transcendental standpoint gave him leverage against commonsense definitions of sanity, enabling him to sunder the linkage between "normality" and "sanity." And with good reason. The tendency to equate normality (or statistical averageness) with sanity or mental health is the result of an elementary philosophical error first noted by Kant. It is desire to confuse the "is" with the "ought." While it is remotely possible that "normality" and "sanity" are identical (or at any rate, convergent), no truly empirical science of the mind would take this proposition on faith. On the contrary, it would begin by weighing and testing the evidence for this claim carefully, and by sedulously disentangling the purely descriptive from the latently prescriptive significations of these terms.

The fact that this has not happened, and is not likely to happen given the current orientation of the mental health professions, suggests a hidden agenda. For the harsher critics of the mental health industry, Laing included, this could be construed as evidence of practitioners' commitment to the project of normalization. Accurate or not, these criticisms may miss the point. Perhaps the tendency to equate normality with mental health, and to conflate the descriptive and prescriptive levels of discourse, is part of a strategy of avoidance and containment, rather than a positive program aimed at enforcing conformity. In other words, perhaps it represents a collective defense mechanism designed to ward off incipient panic and despair. After all, if the majority of people felt that most of their counterparts lack the desire or the ability to discern reality, all trust in consensual systems of belief and the rituals of daily interaction would tend to break down. Even normal people who experience a precipitous drop in "basic trust" are subject to severely anxious, depressive, and/or paranoid reactions. These reactions kindle regressive phantasies, anger, and despair, which in turn foster fears of being mad—fears that escalate as trust in others and the world at large diminishes. (The two invariably go hand in hand.)

So when mental health professionals glibly assume that the normal person is eminently sane, or that sanity *is* normality (and vice versa), they are endorsing a position that spares themselves and others the experience of what Laing, borrowing from Adolph Meyer, termed "psychophobia"—the fear of their own psyche, and more specifically, the dread of being overwhelmed by their own fears and phantasies, perhaps irreversibly. Leaving aside the disparate and contradictory things he said about sanity, Laing's basic project was to "normalize" madness—that is, to make us less afraid of it and more aware of our myriad fears and potentials in that direction. Having brought many lost souls back from the "other side" without recourse to drugs or electroshock, Laing had reason to think that madness may harbor hidden truths, and potentially, hidden benefits.

While Laing's ideas about sanity and the goals of therapy changed, resulting in some deep thematic inconsistencies, there are certain elements that remained constant and constitute both the core of his work and his legacy to posterity. While he wavered on the goals of therapy, for example, he never faltered on the means to achieving a good therapeutic relationship. Despite his eclectic (but judicious) borrowings from various psychodynamic schools, Laing scorned the idea of "technique." But he always regarded empathy; attentiveness; a well-stocked, reliable memory; and a keen sense of humor as the indispensable traits of a good psychotherapist.

Laing also valued "epistemic humility," which is not to be confused with simple modesty. Personal modesty is usually an endearing trait, but a deferential attitude can also cloak considerable grandiosity and unconscious confusion when it comes to the realms of "expert" knowledge. Modesty can incline someone to defer to authority and consensus, to apply the prevailing ideology indiscriminately or in a manner that would please or impress their particular reference group, and to feel "good" for doing so. A really good therapist, by Laing's reckoning, has the lucidity to acknowledge that he or she does not know what is going on. In contrast to Kant and the Enlightenment, whose motto was "Dare to know," Laing said, in effect, dare *not* to. He urged us to cultivate our capacity for wonder, perplexity, and uncertainty, rather than to replace honest doubt with forced categorizations, platitudes, and intellectualization.

For those who work with the deeply disturbed, Laing also required an additional quality—namely, the ability to participate imaginatively in their patients' inner lives by drawing on their own psychotic potential. Though he scoffed at humanistic psychology, Laing was deeply humanistic in the old-fashioned sense, and would have said, with Terence: "I am a man; nothing human is alien to me." For Laing, those who lack this conviction, who cannot sincerely say of their patients "There but for the grace of God go I," have no business working with psychotics.

Another constant and related theme in Laing's work is the appalling absence of the traits he valued in most mental health professionals. In Laing's view, all too many psychiatrists "examine" their patients without truly seeing them. They "assess" a patient's state of mind while ignoring his or her enveloping social context, life history, and worst of all, personal explanations of the source of the distress. Most important, too many psychiatrists discount the possibility that the behavior they observe may be intelligible, even rational, given the extremity of a patient's situation. Thanks to their formidable training, psychiatrists are too tempted to believe that they can stand above these factors and give a quick and "objective" judgment. Psychiatric omniscience, said Laing, is a product of schizoid intellectualization, a splitting of the heart from the mind that pervades the whole culture of psychiatry.

Though Laing waxed eloquent on these abuses, he stopped short of wholesale condemnation. As he told Richard Evans: "I am not putting forward . . . anything like a blanket condemnation of the system, or just saying the easy thing—that the system is entirely self-serving, or the individuals comprising it are self-serving. Our interdigitated plurality of systems is the product of the individuals who compose it, so I am not talking about the system as some entirely alien, malevolent, paranoid-persecution-machine . . . that is devouring everyone in it, though some of us no doubt sometimes feel that way" (in Evans, 1976, p. 37).

Nevertheless, Laing conceded that he felt pretty pessimistic about the future of psychiatry. When Evans prodded him further, Laing went on to note that there is an element of reification inherent in the psychotherapeutic relationship—one rooted in the "cash nexus," or the exchange of services for money. Borrowing from Donald Winnicott, he likened this professional relationship to prostitution. Nevertheless, he continued, what therapists give their clients, in the final analysis, are relationships—and relationships, though treated as commodities by cost-conscious bureaucrats, elude all efforts at precise measurement or control.

Laing felt trends like this should be resisted, but added that psychiatry puts so much emphasis on abilities and aptitudes that are irrelevant to doing effective therapy that the truly desirable traits are now beginning to be "cultured out" of professionals. And much as he regretted it, said Laing, he saw no way of turning back the clock. At the time, more than twenty years ago, his words seemed alarmist. Now they merely seem prophetic. Though he only addressed the issue parenthetically, a serious consideration of Laing's work inevitably prompts the question: Are we witnessing the death of psychotherapy?

Obviously, the answer to that question depends on how we define psychotherapy. The behavioral, cognitive, and cognitive-behavioral approaches flourish now because their time-limited and symptom-focused techniques lend themselves readily to standardization, routinization, and quantification. Though their long-term effectiveness is uncertain, they offer the kinds of treatment that many "consumers" and managed-care "providers" prefer.

So psychotherapy in the sense of symptom remission prospers as psychotherapy in the deeper and broader sense declines. Psychotherapy of this latter sort regards the specific symptoms reported by the patient as expressions of disturbances in the patient's relationship to himself and the world, rather than as nuisances to be eliminated. It regards a patient's suffering not simply as a misfortune, but as an opportunity to wrestle with him or her self—and the therapist—in ways that will eventually deepen his or her insight, dignity, and self-command and give the suffering some redemptive value. As Laing observed, psychotherapy in this sense ultimately entails the provision of a relationship—one that facilitates the experience and expression of as-yet-unintegrated or undeveloped sides of the patient's self.

Some say psychotherapy in this sense is already breathing its last because of the complex interaction between biological psychiatry and managed care. Others think that psychotherapy is merely in critical condition and could be saved with sufficient energy and foresight. But no one who surveys the current state of the mental health professions in the United States can doubt that the future of psychotherapy looks grim (Schneider and Stern, 1997).[2]

Is the possible disappearance of psychotherapy (in the deeper sense) the product of obsolescence or irrelevance, as its critics allege? Is it merely a casualty of economic and market forces? Or are the economic and ideological influences that have mobilized against it indicative of a deeper cultural malaise?

While Laing did not predict the specific features of the current situation, he saw its general outlines emerging quite clearly. Without saying so in quite so many words, Laing suggested to Evans that those who want to quantify, commodify, and control therapy within strict guidelines that are sanctioned and circumscribed by pseudo-medical procedure and terminology are enveloped in different varieties of pseudo-science, though they perforce think that the practitioners who *resist* them are pseudo-scientific.[3] Laing's weary fatalism on this issue did not deter him from speaking out against the rising tide. With the exception of his poetry and two books about his children, everything that Laing published contained pointed reflections on the dangers and abuses of psychiatry and the deepening tendencies toward reification in the mental health professions.

Looking back on this body of work, one inevitably sees problems. A salient one, from our current perspective, is that he did not describe clearly enough the irreducible minimum of reification inherent in the therapeutic relationship. In this age of managed care, when the measurers and managers of psychotherapy services shape, curtail, and define the activities of therapists in the name of science, accountability, and cost-containment, it would be useful to know the proverbial bottom line as a way of rallying clinicians against the intrusive agenda of the nonpractitioners who regulate their relationships to clients. And from a purely phenomenological standpoint, it would have been very useful if Laing had dwelled more on the inherent impossibility of trying to measure an unquantifiable entity like a relationship, and on the varieties of scientism we unwittingly embrace when we collude with those who stubbornly insist on trying to do so.

But if we focus primarily on Laing's logical lapses and omissions, rather than on the issues he raised and the areas where he was admirably consistent, we rapidly lose sight of his real quality and depth. The fact that Laing never presented a single, integrated model of sanity or the therapeutic process is not necessarily grounds for reproach. Laing was not a system builder, and he was not keen to achieve a completely coherent or comprehensive picture of the world. On the contrary, as he told Richard Simon, when he began a book he always started fresh, without attempting to pick up where he had left off. As a result, Laing should be read more in the spirit of Kierkegaard or Nietzsche than of Kraepelin or Freud.

In the final analysis, what we do with Laing's rich and ambiguous legacy is up to us. It would be foolish to discard or forget it. Without minimizing its problems or inconsistencies, let us be thankful for what we have. Perhaps one day when the limitations of biological psychiatry are palpable once more, we can build again on a firmer foundation, inspired in part by his shifting, kaleidoscopic vision. Perhaps.

Fallen Angel (in Memory of R. D. Laing)

Life is luscious. Life is hell.
A ringing, raucous, brazen bell.
Life is longing, love deranged.
Help and hope. But truth is strange.

Searing, sinful, sullen, sad.
Hold it fast, and you'll go mad.
Past imperfect, present tense
Future freighted, lacking sense.

Iffy, irksome, leaden, light.
Boring, spiffy, soaring, trite.
Wholesome, hateful, in-between.
Elemental, lost in dreams.

Life is jumbled, mystic, cross,
Trembling, sacred, found, then lost.
Hegel hiccups. Sartre blinks.
Buddha beckons. Kali winks.

Marx foretells while Nietzsche jeers.
And Freud laments this vale of tears.
Heidegger stutters. Husserl fumes.
And Artaud echoes round the ruins.

Sinews tear midst broken bones.
Severed heads and angry stones.
Missing tongues and vacant eyes.
Hardened hearts that hope despise.

But let us give this life a chance.
And pulse with its demented dance.
Who knows if we've lost our wits?
But wear the shoe, and soon, it fits.

—Daniel Burston

NOTES

BIBLIOGRAPHY

INDEX

· · · N O T E S · · ·

1. An Enigmatic Man

1. I thank Michael Thompson, John Heaton, and Douglas Kirsner for gently calling my attention to previous oversights and omissions in this area.

2. R. D. Laing and Existential Phenomenology

1. Despite Husserl's strictures, Eugene Fink, his leading disciple, eventually conceded that the idea of unconscious mental processes may be defensible from a phenomenological point of view (See appendix 8 to Husserl's *Crisis of the European Sciences,* 1964). For more on the status of the unconscious in phenomenological inquiry, see Chapter 3.

2. I am not the first to note this inconsistency. In *Being and Nothingness* (pt. 4, ch. 2), Sartre noted parenthetically that Heidegger's "classification of 'authentic project' and 'inauthentic project of the self' . . . in spite of its authors intent, is tainted with an ethical concern shown in its very terminology" (Sartre, 1941, p. 721).

3. These two perspectives on consciousness, which I have termed "embedded" and "disembedded," mirror Laing's discussion of the embodied/disembodied self in *The Divided Self.* By treating embodied subjectivity as the "normal" case, Laing indicated his preference for existential phenomenology, though his strictures against dismissing disincarnate spirituality bespeak deep respect for both Husserl and Laing's patients.

3. R. D. Laing and Existential Psychotherapy

1. While derived proximally from the work of Tillich (1952) and Heidegger (1927), Laing's notions of "true" and "false" guilt also bear a close resemblance to humanistic and authoritarian conscience in the work of

Erich Fromm (1947, ch. 4, sec. 2). For more on Heidegger's concept of conscience, see Chapter 4.

2. As another example of a collusive relationship, Laing sometimes cited the relationship between Dora's father and Herr and Frau K in "Fragment of an Analysis of a Case of Hysteria" (Freud, 1905). For a further discussion of this point, see Burston, 1996b, ch. 10.

3. For more on Heidegger and human agency, see Chapter 4.

4. Families, Phenomenology, and Schizophrenia

1. For an illuminating discussion of Laing's knotty relationships with left-wing friends and critics, especially Mitchell, Basaglia, Jacoby, and Sedgwick, see Kotowicz, 1997.

2. The psychiatric imprisonment of women, which was common in the nineteenth century, has not disappeared. But it has diminished appreciably, thanks to the efforts of feminist and human rights advocates who have called attention to these abuses (e.g., Packard, 1873; Chesler, 1972; Showalter, 1985; Caplan, 1995).

3. The role of transference in the training of mental health professionals has been addressed by psychoanalysis, albeit seldom satisfactorily. In most quarters, this phenomenon still goes by the generic name of "suggestion," and has been neglected since the groundbreaking studies of Temerlin, 1968, and Temerlin and Trousdale, 1969. In "Suggestion Effects in Psychiatric Diagnosis," Temerlin (1968) demonstrated how the perceptions and pronouncements of authority figures assessing patients bias the clinical judgment of less senior or experienced practitioners, and how susceptibility to such influence (and corresponding distortions in judgment) increases with the number of years the person has been trained or socialized into the psychiatric profession. The upshot of Temerlin's study appears to be that increased training diminishes, rather than enhances, independent judgment—a depressing conclusion for practitioners and "consumers" alike.

4. For more on this point, see Chapter 5.

5. In *The Divided Self* (1960), Laing discusses the role and meaning of imitation in schizoid adults very perceptively. But, these remarks about "James," "Peter," and so on apply to a specific group of disturbed adults—not to relatively intact children, whose imitative play has a different source and function. Laing came nearest to acknowledging the agentic dimension of childhood imitation in *Wisdom, Madness and Folly,* in the case of "Nan," a brain-damaged teenager whose prior socialization and personality were completely erased by a near fatal car ac-

cident that left her comatose for several months. During her recovery, Nan acquired a totally different personality than the one she had possessed prior to her accident: one, said Laing, that began as "a construction of the others," but evolved dialectically into an ensemble of traits and behaviors that she used effectively to negotiate and achieve her own ends (Laing, 1985; Burston, 1996, pp. 39–40). Laing did not mention imitation specifically, but his impressions of the gradual resocialization of this young woman imply an awareness of the active role a person takes in forming and negotiating his or her own personality in the face of others' designs.

5. Normality and the Numinous

1. For a very similar perspective, see Perry, 1974.
2. For a very different assessment of Heidegger's views on human agency, see Theodor Itten's "An Investigation into Labor, Work and Artistic Creation in Relation to Psychotherapy with Reference to the Philosophy of Martin Heidegger" (unpublished, on file with the author, 1992).
3. For an illuminating discussion of this point, see Rockmore, 1995, ch. 6.
4. Recent transactions between Swiss banks, the Swiss government, the Swiss media, and Holocaust survivors underscore how deep and widespread anti-Semitism was—and still is—among Jung's compatriots, and how much collaboration and complicity were concealed behind the cloak of neutrality during the war. But Jung's anti-Semitism was of a very peculiar kind because it was profoundly affected by his conflicts with Freud, a relationship that intensified his earlier Gnostic leanings (Burston, 1999). For illuminating documentation and discussion of Jung's Nazi sympathies from a Jungian perspective, see Maidenbaum and Martin, 1991; Samuels, 1993; Adams, 1996. For a splendid discussion of the phenomenological dimension of Jung's theory, see Roger Brooke's *Jung and Phenomenology* (1991).
5. Despite my best efforts, I simply cannot comprehend a school of thought that claims unwavering fidelity to Freud while simultaneously espousing a conciliatory attitude to organized religion, and for that very reason, in many instances, proscribing some of Freud's most important books, including *Totem and Taboo, The Ego and the Id, The Future of an Illusion,* and *Civilization and Its Discontents*. If Lacan and his followers insist on being so selective and sectarian in their reading of Freud, it would be more honest and economical of them to make a candid avowal of their revisionist intentions, rather than perpetuate this transparent charade.
6. The exception, of course, is Jean Piaget, whose genetic structuralism pre-

serves the concept of an epistemic subject, a locus of experience and intentions toward the world—albeit a decentered (and by implication, unconscious) one (Piaget, 1970; 1976). Clinicians engaged with post-structuralist, deconstructionist, and postmodern discourse really ought to pay more attention to his thinking on the "cognitive unconscious" (see Burston, 1986a).

7. My admittedly schematic descriptions of the Gnostic and Messianic mentalities lean on Tillich's discussion of the Judaic and Hellenistic elements in Christianity (1968), on Fromm's discussion of the Messianic mind (e.g., Fromm, 1961; Burston, 1991), and on Hans Jonas's impressive body of work on Gnosticism (1952; 1963; 1974). Like Jonas, I think Gershom Scholem was profoundly mistaken when he characterized Kabalah as "Jewish Gnosticism." Strictly speaking, there is no such thing (Jonas, 1974, ch. 14). Nevertheless, Gnostic tropes do work their way into Jewish mysticism via kindred elements in the neo-Platonic corpus, and eventually resurface in Hasidism, which effects a curious and compelling synthesis of these hitherto antagonistic mentalities (minus the characteristic anti-Semitism of the original Gnostics).

6. R. D. Laing and the Crisis of Psychotherapy

1. During his tenure as president of the American Psychological Association from 1998 to 1999, Dr. Martin Seligman openly deplored the fact that psychology is focused on diagnosing and treating pathology and not interested in understanding and promoting mental health. While I applaud his efforts to reverse this situation, I wonder if it is wise to single out psychology in this way. Is it uniquely qualified to make progress in this regard, as Seligman contends? If so, perhaps, the other mental health professions can continue being complacent on this score. In fairness to Seligman, he may have thought it impolitic to lecture other disciplines on their mission or their inherent limitations. But if psychology is to claim special competence in this area, it will have to demonstrate such competence first, and at present is still far from achieving this goal.

2. The emerging crisis of psychotherapy is discussed with considerable insight in Aanstoos, 1994; Schneider, 1995; Wertz, 1995; Fensterheim and Raw, 1996; O'Hara, 1997; Bohart, Leitner, and O'Hara, 1998; and Schneider, 1998.

3. Despite a promising beginning with Evans, to my knowledge Laing never discussed elsewhere the problems engendered by the attempt to quantify and commodify relationships in connection with therapy. But he did take up similar issues in related contexts. For example, in 1980 Laing admon-

ished psychotherapy researcher Roberta Russell, who was attempting to engage him in co-counseling, not to confuse feelings with commodities, and not to introduce marketing metaphors into the psychology of love and interpersonal attraction (Russell, 1992, ch. 17). And in 1987, reflecting on methodological issues, he alluded to the ineradicable element of mystery and uncertainty that accompanies interpersonal processes: "There is so much that goes on between us which we can never know. The necessity of this ignorance, and the impossibility of any satisfactory criteria of decidability when it comes to the validation of particular attributions of a personal or interpersonal order, have led those who wish to cultivate the art of the soluble to abandon this area of uncertainty and enigmas. However, this domain does not evaporate because the objective look does not see it" (Laing, 1987, p. 418).

· · · BIBLIOGRAPHY · · ·

Aanstoos, C. 1994. "Mainstream Psychology and the Humanistic Alternative." Pp. 1–11 in *The Humanistic Movement: Recovering the Person in Psychology*, ed. F. J. Wertz. Lake Worth, Fla.: Gardner.

Abrams, M. H. 1971. *Natural Supernaturalism: Tradition and Revolution in Romantic Literature*. New York: W. W. Norton.

Adams, M. V. 1996. *The Multicultural Imagination: "Race," Color and the Unconscious*. London: Routledge.

Arendt, H. 1978. *The Life of the Mind*. New York: Harcourt, Brace, Jovanovich.

Armstrong, T. 1997. *The Myth of the A.D.D. Child*. New York: Plume Books.

Avnon, D. 1998. *Martin Buber: The Hidden Dialogue*. New York: Rowman and Littlefield.

Bateson, G., and D. Lackson, J. Haley, and J. Weakland, 1968. "Toward a Theory of Schizophrenia." In *Communication, Family and Marriage*. Palo Alto. Science and Behavior Books.

Benjamin, J. 1988. *The Bonds of Love: Psychoanalysis, Feminism and The Problem of Domination*. New York: Pantheon.

Berke, J. 1990. "R. D. Laing: An Appreciation." *British Journal of Psychiatry*. 7, no. 2.

Bloch, E. 1972. *Atheism in Christianity*. New York: Herder & Herder.

Bohart, A., L. Leitner, and M. O'Hara. 1998. "Empirically Violated Treatments: Disenfranchisement of Humanistic and Other Approaches." *Psychotherapy Research*, 8, 141–157.

Borch-Jakobsen, M. 1991, *Lacan: The Absolute Master*. Stanford, Calif.: Stanford University Press.

Boss, M. 1963. *Daseinanalysis and Psychoanalysis*. New York: Basic Books.

Boss, M. 1977. "Martin Heidegger's Zollikon Seminars," Reprinted in *Review of Existential Psychology and Psychiatry* 16, nos. 1, 2, and 3 (1988).

Bowlby, J. 1988. *A Secure Base*. London: Routledge.

Breggin, P. 1991. *Toxic Psychiatry*. New York: St. Martin's.

Bronner, S. 1994. *Of Critical Theory and Its Theorists*. Oxford: Basil Blackwell.

Brooke, R. 1991. *Jung and Phenomenology*. London: Routledge.

Brown, P. 1990 "The Name Game: Toward a Sociology of Diagnosis." *Journal of Mind and Behavior* 2, nos. 3 and 4, pp. 139–160.

Buber, M. 1923. *I and Thou*. Trans. Ronald Gregor Smith. New York: Charles Scribner's Sons, 1958.

Buber, M. 1947. *Between Man and Man*. Trans. Ronald Gregor Smith. Boston: Beacon Press, 1955.

Buber, M. 1957. *Eclipse of God: Studies in the Relation Between Religion and Philosophy*. Trans. M. Friedman, New York: Harper Torchbooks.

Buber, M. 1964. *The Knowledge of Man*. Ed. Maurice Freidman. New York: Harper.

Burston, D. 1986. "The Cognitive and Dynamic Unconscious: A Critical and Historical Perspective." *Contemporary Psychoanalysis* 22, no. 1, pp. 133–157.

Burston, D. 1991. *The Legacy of Erich Fromm*. Cambridge: Harvard University Press.

Burston, D. 1992, "Psychiatric Sophistry: A Review of Laurie Rezneck's *The Philosophical Defense of Psychiatry*." *Contemporary Psychology* 37, no. 9.

Burston, D., 1996a. *The Wing of Madness: The Life and Work of R. D. Laing*. Cambridge: Harvard University Press.

Burston, D. 1996b. "Conflict and Sociability in Hegel, Freud and Their Followers." *New Literary History*. 27, no. 1, pp. 73–82.

Burston, D. 1999. "Archetype and Interpretation." *Psychoanalytic Review* 86, no. 1, pp. 35–62.

Burston, D. and S. Olfman. 1996. "Freud, Fromm and the Pathology of Normalcy." In *A Prophetic Analyst: Reclaiming Fromm's Legacy*, ed. M. Cortina and M. Maccoby. New York: Aronson.

Canguilhem, G. 1966. *The Normal and the Pathological*. Trans. C. Fawcett, intro M. Foucault. New York: Zone Books, 1989.

Caplan. P. 1995. *They Say You're Crazy*. New York: Addison-Wesley.

Chesler, P. 1975. *Women and Madness*. New York: Harcourt, Brace, Jovanovich.

Clay, J. 1996. *R. D. Laing: A Divided Self*. London: Hodder & Stoughton.

Cohn, H. 1994. "What Is Existential Psychotherapy?" *British Journal of Psychiatry* 165, pp. 699–701.

Cohn, N. 1970. *The Pursuit of the Millenium*. New York: Oxford University Press.

Connerton, P., ed. 1978. *Critical Sociology: Selected Readings.* Harmondsworth: Penguin Books.

Cooper, D. 1967a. *Psychiatry and Anti-Psychiatry.* London: Tavistock.

Cooper, D., ed. 1967b. *The Dialectics of Liberation.* Harmondsworth: Penguin.

Cooper, D. 1971. *The Death of the Family.* New York: Vintage Books.

Dilthey, W. 1989. *Introduction to the Human Sciences,* ed. R. Makkreel and F. Rodi. Princeton, N.J.: Princeton University Press.

Evans, R. 1976. *R. D. Laing: The Man and His Ideas.* New York: E. P. Dutton.

Fackenheim, E. 1970. *The Religious Dimension in Hegel's Thought.* Boston: Beacon Press.

Fanon, F. 1967. *Black Skins. White Masks.* Trans. C. L. Markmann. New York: Grove Press.

Fensterheim, H., and S. D. Raw. 1996. "Psychotherapy Research Is Not Psychotherapy Practice." *Clinical Psychology: Science and Practice* 3, pp. 168–171.

Fort, D. C. 1990. "Parent-Child Effects on Performance, Thinking and Communication in Families of Normal and Schizophrenic Sons." *Journal of the American Academy of Psychoanalysis* 18, no. 1, pp. 73–98.

Frank, J. A. 1990. "Listening with the Big Ear: A Laingian Approach to Psychotic Families." *Journal of the American Academy of Psychoanalysis* 18, no. 1, pp. 131–144.

Freud, S. 1905. *Fragment of An Analysis of A Case of Hysteria.* Vol. 7 in *The Standard Edition of the Complete Psychological Works of Sigmund Freud,* ed. James Strachey. 24 vols. London: Hogarth Press, 1953–1974.

Friedman, M. 1989. "Intersubjectivity in Husserl, Sartre, Heidegger and Buber." *Review of Existential Psychology and Psychiatry* 21, nos. 1, 2, and 3, pp. 63–80.

Friedman, M., ed. 1994. *Worlds of Existentialism.* Atlantic Highlands, N.J.: Humanities Paperback Library.

Fromm, E. 1941. *Escape From Freedom.* Reprint, New York: Avon Books, 1965.

Fromm, E. 1947. *Man for Himself: An Inquiry into the Psychology of Ethics.* New York: Holt, Rinehart and Winston.

Fromm, E. 1955. *The Sane Society.* Greenwich, Conn.: Fawcett Premier Books.

Fromm, E. 1956. *The Art of Loving.* Reprint, New York: Bantam Books, 1970.

Fromm, E. 1961. *Marx's Concept of Man.* New York: Frederick Ungar.

Fromm, E. 1964. *The Heart of Man: Its Genius for Good and Evil.* Reprint, New York: Harper & Row, 1968.

Fromm, E. 1970. *The Crisis of Psychoanalysis.* Greenwich, Conn.: Fawcett Premier Books.

Fromm, E. 1980. *Greatness and Limitations of Freud's Thought.* New York: Harper & Row.

Fromm, E. 1992. *The Revision of Psychoanalysis.* Boulder, Colo.: Westview Press.

Fromm, E., D. T. Suzuki, and R. DeMartino. 1960. *Zen Buddhism and Psychoanalysis.* New York: Harper & Row.

Gadamer, H. G. 1976. *Philosophical Hermeneutics.* Trans D. Inge. Berkeley: University of California Press.

Goffman, I. 1961. *Asylums: Essays on the Social Situation of Asylum Patients and Other Inmates.* Chicago: Aldine.

Gordon, J. 1990. "Visionary Who Always Saw the Individual: R. D. Laing Remembered." *Psychiatric Times.* (April).

Hegel, G. W. F. 1807. *The Phenomenology of Mind.* Trans J. B. Baille, intro G. Lichtheim. New York: Harper Torchbooks, 1967.

Heidegger, M. 1927. *Being and Time.* Trans. J. Macquarrie. New York: Harper * Row, 1962.

Heidegger, M. 1949. "Letter on Humanism." In M. Friedman, *Worlds of Existentialism.* Atlantic Highlands, N.J.: Humanities Press, 1994.

Heidegger, M. 1982. *Parmendies.* Trans A. Schuwer and R. Rojcewicz. Bloomington: Indiana University Press, 1992.

Hothersall, D. 1995. *History of Psychology.* New York: McGraw Hill.

Husserl, E., 1960. *Cartesian Meditations. An Introduction to Phenomenology.* Trans. D. Cairns. The Hague: Martinus Nijhoff.

Husserl, E., 1970. *The Crisis of the European Sciences and Transcendental Phenomenology.* Trans D. Carr, Evanston, Ill.: Northwestern University Press.

Hyppolite, J. 1946, *Genesis and Structure of Hegel's Phenomenology of Spirit.* Trans. J. Heckman, Evanston, Ill.: Northwestern University Press, 1974.

Itten, T. 1992. "An Investigation into Labour, Work and Artistic Creation in Relation to Psychotherapy with Reference to the Philosophy of Martin Heidegger." Master's thesis, Dept. of Social Science and Humanities, City University, London.

Jaspers, K. 1913. *General Psychopathology.* Chicago: University of Chicago Press:

Jonas, H., 1963. *The Gnostic Religions.* Boston: Beacon Press.

Jonas, H. 1974. *Philosophical Essays.* Chicago: University of Chicago Press.

Jung, C. G. 1933. *Modern Man in Search of a Soul.* New York: Harcourt, Brace, Jovanovich, 1960.

Jung, C. G. 1935. *Analytical Psychology: Its Theory and Practice.* New York: Vintage Books, 1968.

Jung, C. G., ed. 1964. *Man and His Symbols.* London: Aldus Books.

Kierkegaard, S. 1855. *An Attack Upon Christendom.* Trans. W. Lowrie. Princeton, N.J.: Princeton University Press, 1944.

Kirk, S., and H. Kutchins. 1992. *The Selling of DSM: The Rhetoric of Science in Psychiatry.* Hawthorne, N.Y.: Aldine de Gruyter.

Kirshner, S. 1996. *The Religious and Romantic Origins of Psychoanalysis.* Cambridge: Cambridge University Press.

Kirsner, D. 1976. *The Schizoid World of Jean-Paul Sartre and R. D. Laing.* Brisbane: University of Queensland Press.

Kockelmans, J. 1988. "Daseinanalysis and Freud's Unconscious." *Review of Existential Psychology and Psychiatry* 16, nos. 1, 2, and 3.

Kojeve, A. 1969. *An Introduction to the Reading of Hegel.* Ed R. Queneau. Ithaca, N.Y.: Cornell University Press.

Kotowicz, Z. 1997. *R. D. Laing and the Paths of Anti-Psychiatry.* London: Routledge.

Lacan, J. 1978. *The Four Fundamental Concepts of Psychoanalysis.* Trans. Alan Sheridan. New York: W. W. Norton.

Laing, R. D. 1994. *R. D. Laing: A Biography.* London: Peter Owen.

Laing, R. D. 1960. *The Divided Self.* London: Tavistock Publications. Harmondsworth: Penguin, 1990.

Laing, R. D. 1961. *Self and Others: Further Studies in Sanity and Madness.* London: Tavistock Publications. Harmondsworth: Penguin, 1990.

Laing, R. D. 1963a. "Minkowski and Schizophrenia." *Review of Existential Psychology and Psychiatry* 3, no. 3.

Laing, R. D., 1963b. "Review of *Schizophrenia as a Human Process* by H. S. Sullivan." *International Journal of Psychoanalysis* 44, no. 3.

Laing, R. D. 1964. "Review of *General Psychopathology* by Karl Jaspers." *International Journal of Psychoanalysis,* 45, no. 4.

Laing, R. D. 1967. *"The Politics of Experience" and "The Bird of Paradise."* New York: Pantheon.

Laing, R. D. 1968. "The Obvious." In *The Dialectics of Liberations,* ed. D. Cooper. Harmondsworth: Penguin.

Laing, R. D. 1969. *Self and Others.* Rev. ed. Harmondsworth: Penguin.

Laing, R. D. 1970. *Knots.* New York: Pantheon.

Laing, R. D. 1971. *"Politics of the Family" and Other Essays.* New York: Pantheon.

Laing, R. D. 1976. *The Facts of Life.* New York: Pantheon.

Laing, R. D. 1982. *The Voice of Experience.* New York: Pantheon.

Laing, R. D. 1985. *Wisdom, Madness and Folly: The Making of a Psychiatrist.* New York: McGraw Hill.

Laing, R. D. 1987. "Laing's Understanding of Interpersonal Experience." In *The Oxford Companion to the Mind,* ed. Richard Gregory. New York: Oxford University Press.

Laing, R. D., and D. Cooper. 1964. *Reason and Violence: A Decade of Sartre's Philosophy*. New York: Pantheon.

Laing, R. D. and A. Esterson. 1964. *Sanity, Madness and the Family*. London: Tavistock Publications. Reprint, Harmondsworth: Penguin, 1990.

Laing, R. D., H. Phillipson, and A. R. Lee. 1966. *Interpersonal Perception: A Theory and Method of Research*. London: Tavistock Publications.

Leff, J., and C. Vaughn. 1985. *Expressed Emotion in Families*. New York: Guilford Press.

MacMurray, J. 1957. *Self as Agent*. London: Faber & Faber.

Maidenbaum, A., and S. Martin. 1991. *Lingering Shadows: Freudians, Jungians, and Anti-Semitism*. Boston: Shambala Press.

Makkreel, R. 1975. *Dilthey: Philosopher of the Human Sciences*. Princeton, N.J.: Princeton University Press.

Mead, G. H. 1934. *Mind, Self and Society*. Chicago: University of Chicago Press.

Merleau-Ponty, M. 1942. *The Structure of Behavior*. Trans. Alden Fisher, Boston: Beacon Books, 1963.

Merleau-Ponty, M. 1964. *The Primacy of Perception*. Ed J. Wild, Evanston, Ill.: Northwestern University Press.

Mesulam, M. 1990. "Schizophrenia and the Brain." *New England Journal of Medicine*. 322, no. 12, pp. 842–845.

Mill, J. S. 1858. "The Law of Lunacy." In J. Robson and A. Robson, eds., *Collected Works of John Stuart Mill: Newspaper Writings, January 1835–June 1847*. Toronto: University of Toronto Press, 1986.

Mirandola, P. D. 1494. "On the Dignity of Man." In *"On The Dignity of Man," "On Being and the One," "Heptaplus,"* trans. C. G. Wallis, P. J. W. Miller, and D. Carmichael. New York: Bobbs-Merrill, 1965.

Mirowsky, J. and C. Ross. 1989. "Psychiatric Diagnosis as Reified Measurement." *Journal of Health and Social Behavior* 30, pp. 11–25.

Moldin, S. O. and I. I. Gottesman. 1997. "Genes, Experience and Chance in Schizophrenia: Positioning for the Twenty-first Century." *Schizophrenia Bulletin* 23, no. 4, pp. 547–561

Morel, B. A. 1860. *Traites des maladies mentales*. Paris: Librairie Victor Masson.

Mullan, B. 1995. *Mad to Be Normal. Conversations with R. D. Laing*. London: Free Association.

Mullan, B. 1997. *R. D. Laing: Creative Destroyer*. London: Cassell.

Muller, R. 1979. Interview with R. D. Laing, October 5, Capitol Hilton Hotel, Washington, D. C. On file with the author.

Nietzsche, F. 1887. *The Geneology of Morals*. Trans. F. Golfing. New York: Anchor Books, 1956.

O'Hara, M. 1997. "Emancipatory Therapeutic Practice in a Turbulent Trans-modern Era: A Work of Retrieval." *Journal of Humanistic Psychology* 37, no. 3, pp. 7–33.

O'Neill, J., ed. 1996. *Hegel's Dialectic of Desire and Recognition.* Albany: State University of New York Press.

Packard, E. 1873, *Modern Persecution, or Insane Asylums Unveiled.* New York: Pelletreau & Raynor.

Perry, J. W., 1974. *The Far Side of Madness.* Dallas: Spring Publications.

Piaget, J. 1970. *Structuralism.* New York: Basic Books.

Piaget, J. 1976. *The Child and Reality.* Harmondsworth: Penguin.

Poster, M. 1980. *Critical Theory of the Family.* New York: Continuum.

Ricoeur, P. 1970. *Freud and Philosophy: An Essay on Interpretation.* New Haven: Yale University Press.

Rockmore, T. 1993. "Aspects of French Hegelianism," *The Owl of Minerva* 24, no. 2, pp. 191–206.

Rockmore, T. 1995. *Heidegger and French Philosophy: Humanism, Anti-Humanism and Being.* London: Routledge.

Rosen, G. 1968. *Madness in Society.* New York: Harper & Row.

Rosenhan, D. 1973. "On Being Sane In Insane Places," *Science,* 179, pp. 250–258.

Russell, R., 1992. *R. D. Laing and Me: Lessons in Love.* Lake Placid: Hilgarth Press.

Rycroft, C. 1968. *A Critical Dictionary of Psychoanalysis.* Harmondsworth: Penguin Books.

Rycroft, C. 1973. "On the Ablation of Parental Images, or The Illusion of Having Created Oneself." Reprinted in *Psychoanalysis and Beyond,* ed. P. Fuller. Chicago: University of Chicago Press, 1985.

Samuels, A. 1993. "New Material Concerning Jung, Anti-Semitism and the Nazis." *Journal of Analytical Psychology* 38, pp. 463–470.

Sartre, J-P. 1936. "Transcendence of the Ego." Reprinted in *Hegel's Dialectic of Desire and Recognition,* ed. J. O'Neill. Albany: State University of New York Press, 1996.

Sartre, J-P. 1941. *Being and Nothingness.* Trans H. Barnes, New York: Washington Square Press, 1956.

Sass, L. 1986. "Humanism, Hermeneutics and the Concept of the Human Subject." In *Hermeneutics and Psychological Theory: Interpretive Perspectives on Personality, Psychotherapy and Psychopathology,* ed. S. Messer, A. Sass, and R. Woolfolk. New Brunswick, N.J.: Rutgers University Press.

Sass, L. 1992. *Madness and Modernism: Insanity in the Light of Modern Art Literature and Thought.* New York: Basic Books.

Scheler, M. 1913. *The Nature of Sympathy.* Trans. P. Heath. Hamden, Conn.: Archon Books, 1970.

Scheler, M. 1915a. *Ressentiment.* Trans. L. Coser and W. Holdheim. Milwaukee, Wis.: Marquette University Press, 1994.

Scheler, M. 1915b. "The Idols of Self-Knowledge." In *Max Scheler: Selected Philosophical Essays,* trans. D. Lachterman, Evanston, Ill.: Northwestern University Press, 1973.

Schneider, K., and R. May. 1995. *The Psychology of Existence: An Integrative, Clinical Perspective.* New York: McGraw-Hill.

Schneider, K., and M. Stern. 1997. "Report from the Front." Newsletter of division 32 of The American Psychological Association, (Summer), pp. 2–4.

Schneider, K. 1998. "Toward a Science of the Heart: Romanticism and the Revival of Psychology." *American Psychologist* 53, no. 3.

Schneiderman, S., 1984. *Jacques Lacan: The Death of An Intellectual Hero.* Cambridge: Harvard University Press.

Sedgewick, P. 1980. *Psychopolitics.* London: Pluto Press.

Segal, R., ed. 1992. *The Gnostic Jung.* Princeton, N.J.: Princeton University Press.

Sigal, C. 1976. *Zone of the Interior.* New York: Crowell.

Simon, R. 1983. "Still R. D. Laing after All These Years." *Family Therapy Networker* 7, no. 3.

Showalter, E. 1985. *The Female Malady: Women, Madness and English Culture, 1830–1980.* Harmondsworth: Penguin Books.

Skrabanek, P. 1997. "From Language to Lesion." *Review of Existential Psychology and Psychiatry* 23, nos. 1, 2, and 3.

Soper, K. 1986. *Humanism and Anti-Humanism.* La Salle, Ill.: Open Court Books.

Stern, D. 1985. *The Interpersonal World of the Infant: A View from Psychoanalysis and Developmental Psychology.* New York: Basic Books.

Stewart, D. and A. Mickunas. 1974. *Exploring Phenomenology: A Guide to the Field and Its Literature.* Athens: Ohio University Press.

Storr, A. 1977. "Laing: The Painful birth of a Theory." *Sunday Times* (London), Nov. 21.

Suttie, A. 1935. *The Origins of Love and Hate.* London: Pelican Books.

Temerlin, M. 1968. "Suggestion Effects in Psychiatric Diagnosis." *Journal of Mental and Nervous Disease* 147, no. 4, pp. 349–353.

Temerlin, M., and W. Trousdale. 1969. "The Social Psychology of Clinical Diagnosis." *Psychotherapy: Theory, Research and Practice.* 6, pp. 24–29.

Tillich, P. 1968. *A History of Christian Thought.* New York: Simon & Schuster.

Tillich, P. 1975. *The Courage To Be.* New Haven: Yale University Press.

Walsh, R. 1996. "The Problem of Unconsciousness in Qualitative Research." *British Journal of Guidance and Counselling* 24, no. 3, pp. 377–384.

Wertz, F. J. 1995. "The Scientific Status of Psychology." *Humanistic Psychologist* 23, no. 3, pp. 285–304.

Nazism, 14, 116, 117, 119, 131
Nietzsche, F., 3, 12, 14, 21, 23, 34, 113, 116–117, 118, 130, 146
normality: and the atrophy of the numinous, 107; as "deficiency disease," 103, 127; and depersonalization of others (Laing), 104; and ontological security, 104, 135–136; as pseudosanity, 7, 48, 106, 119, 135; and social phantasy systems, 104–105, 114; vs. mental health, 132, 141. *See also* mental health
normality, models of: cultural, 99; medical, 99–100; psychopathological, 100–101; statistical, 98–99
normalization, 59, 86–87, 114. *See also* psychotherapy: goals of

Oedipus complex, 89, 90
ontological (in)security, 3, 37, 134–138
optimism/pessimism (in Laing), 48–50

Packard, E., 64
phenomenology, 16, 77; existential, 29–30; and Jungian psychology, 121, 153; and psychoanalysis, 23–26, 84–88; social, 74–83, 121–122
phenomenology, transcendental, 16–20, 78–79; and *epoche*, 17, 78; and idealism, 19; and natural and theoretical attitudes, 17–19, 136; and solipsism, 23, 30
Philadelphia Association, 6, 8, 10, 11
Piaget, J., 153–154
Pinel, P., 63
Plato, 128; neo-platonism, 110, 128
Poster, M., 58
pretence, 41–42
psychosis: and absence of recognition, 31, 39; as existential crisis, 6, 70; as loss of conventional social filters, 5; and unlivable situations, 60
psychotherapy: birth-oriented, 9, 10, 42, 50; cognitive-behavioral, 144–145; goals of, 7, 35, 36, 39, 47, 51–52, 122, 137, 144; group therapy, 45–47; quantifiable and nonquantifiable factors in, 35, 36, 144–145, 154–155; reification in, 54, 143–144; and sha-

manism, 106; supervision of, 55–56; techniques of, 36, 38–39, 52, 54–55, 142; transformation in, 26
psychotherapy cases and/or clinical vignettes: anonymous agoraphobic, 41; anonymous writer, 44; Antoine, 64; David Clark, 92–93; Edward, 89; Hans, 67–69; Henry, 60–62; Julie, 79; Mrs. A, 71; Mrs. D., 38; Nan, 152–153; Peter and Rose, 40

Rank, O., 9
Redler, L., 56
repression, 105, 123–124
Rezneck, J., 11
Ricoeur, P., 14, 30
Rockmore, T., 31
Rogers, C., 33, 34, 37, 39, 54
Romayn-Kendon, M., 11
Rosenhan, D., 62–63
Rush, B., 63
Rycroft, C., 5, 94–96

Sass, L., 72
Sartre, J-P., 5, 14, 15, 16, 29, 31, 41, 79–82, 85, 87, 95–96, 120, 123, 125, 151
Scheler, M., 20, 23, 24, 41
schizophrenia: and "expressed emotion," 76; and family research, 78–91; and genetic predisposition to, 72–73; intelligibility of, 65–70, 88–90; as a neurobiological disorder, 71; splitting in, 42
Schneiderman, S., 86
Schorstein, J., 4, 119, 128–129
secularization, 107, 129
self: in Jung, 125; in Lacan, 123; in Laing, 123–126; in Sartre, 123, 125; in Winnicott, 125. *See also* agency; consciousness
self-authorship: individual, 33–34; collective, 111
self-consciousness, emergence of, 50–51
self-deception, 23–24, 25, 35, 41, 42, 87, 118
self-disclosure, 37, 44
self-knowledge: in Hegel, 110–111; in Heidegger, 25–26, 111–113; in Husserl, 24